The Autopilot
Leadership Model

The Autopilot
Leadership Model

SAMMY LEE

Mc
Graw
Hill
Education

THE AUTOPILOT LEADERSHIP MODEL

Cover design by Lee Meng Hui.

10 9 8 7 6 5 4 3 2 1
20 18 17 16

When ordering this title, use **ISBN 978-9-814-74255-9** or **MHID 9-814-74255-4**

Printed in China

FOREWORD by Professor John A. Davis

In *Autopilot Leadership*, successful entrepreneur Sammy Lee distills generations of wisdom about leadership and building a great company from his experience as founder of Infinitus and member of the third generation sibling team that owns and leads his family's Hong Kong sauce business, Lee Kum Kee. The result of Sammy Lee's work is undeniably impressive: Infinitus has grown more than 180 times in 16 years and has been named as the best company to work for in China and in Asia.

Sammy Lee's inspiring and useful book shows how companies can thrive and grow by taking *very* good care of their employees and customers—and their leaders. Caring about the welfare of one's stakeholders and helping them lead healthy, satisfying lives is not a platitude for Sammy Lee; it is a way of life that he and his Infinitus colleagues practice everyday. And it is fair to say that the principles of *Autopilot Leadership* not only saved his company, Infinitus; it saved Sammy's life.

Business leaders talk a lot about responding to stakeholders' needs concerning their business, but they don't necessarily take this principle to the next level—taking an interest in their lives. At Infinitus, caring for stakeholders means building a healthy company that contributes to the physical, social, psychological and spiritual health of everyone around it. To do that, people working at Infinitus (not just Sammy, the company leader) engage compassionately with one another and support company programs to help one another be productive and healthy at work and also lead healthy lives in general. Infinitus promotes the Three Balances of Life: Health, Family and Work. Sammy Lee demonstrates in his absorbing, timely book what a principles-based "humanistic capitalism" looks like and how it benefits employees, leaders, owners and society.

In a compelling style, Sammy also describes his personal struggle as an entrepreneur. He relates how he learned to trust the *"Invisible Leader"* tenets of Lao Zi to be able to increase his care for himself and his managers and employees. This allowed Sammy to rise above operational issues (reducing his stress and improving his health) and focus his leadership on building a vital organization with strong values and loyalty that could grow and become a model company. Infinitus employees actually assess and discuss with one another their level of happiness.

The humanistic approach espoused in *Autopilot Leadership* is an elevated form of doing good and is just one way of running a company. But *Autopilot Leadership* is a powerful form of capitalism that I hope will become more popular with owners and leaders of companies because it not only produces exceptional business results but also attracts and retains exceptional employees. Researchers around the world are paying increasing attention to this business approach of "doing well while doing good."

I'm particularly fascinated with Infinitus and Sammy Lee's leadership because this is a family-owned and led company, which is my research and advisory specialty. It's not surprising that the Lee family is behind this innovative enterprise. Studies confirm that family companies perform better, care more for their stakeholders and are more trusted than any other type of business. But *Autopilot Leadership* is an approach that can transform every company.

Read this book and understand what Sammy Lee has discovered about building a great company. It just may inspire you to build a healthy culture in your own business; and it just may save your life.

John Davis
Faculty Chair, Families in Business Program
Harvard Business School
Boston, Massachusetts

FOREWORD by Professor John L. Ward

As a student of family business I have long been keenly interested in what it takes, especially in the form of leadership, to build a long-lasting institution—an institution that can renovate itself over and over again. I have found that those very, very few family successor leaders who have recreated their businesses when faced with market change and organizational maturity can do so only once in their career.

To me, doing so is a tremendous achievement and those leaders are excellent strategists and managers of people and are to be commended for sustaining their companies for another life cycle.

Yet today for companies to endure in most industries, it requires renovation over and over, often every five to seven years, as life cycles of success grow shorter and shorter. Business leaders who can do that, I find, are extraordinarily rare and I find them the most fascinating of leaders. After all, they have to be motivated by more than social status and financial rewards as they have already achieved those things. In fact, by staying with their enterprises for ever more strategic and organizational recreations they are perpetually risking all they have earned by continuing as the guardian of the institution they treasure. And, we know, most authors of a success formula are unable to see the limits of the paradigm they have invented.

So, I relish the search for and study of such leaders who are able to perpetuate the magnificence of an institution through decades of challenge and change. What motivates them? How do they lead?

I find several common characteristics:

- They set an indefinite mission for their enterprise—to continue forever.
- They are active "in the world of ideas"; they are willing to put their beliefs on trial with the most challenging thinkers.

- They are stewards of capital—believing the rewards of success belong to the institution and the future of that institution.
- They seek to build a durable and self-sustaining philosophy of management; that is their most personally compelling entrepreneurial innovation—though always incomplete.

Sammy Lee is a role model of this type of leader. His purpose is the business continuity of his family's business. He craves to learn from critics. He embraces the dignity of people and the responsibility to all stakeholders. *Autopilot Leadership* is an inspiring philosophy of management.

There are features of *Autopilot Leadership* I find most unique from among the rare universe of management-leader-philosophers:

- The purpose of "happiness."
- The joy of investing in people's personal growth.
- The foundation value of trust.
- The melding of tradition and innovation and of Eastern philosophy and Western enterprise.

This book will inspire those who value the legacy of enduring institutions.

John L. Ward
Clinical Professor of Family Enterprises
Kellogg School of Management
Chicago, USA

Acknowledgments

Since I was a child, I frequently accompanied my father to attend funerals. Whenever the master of ceremony read out the deceased's eulogy, it always came across as report card. The achievements of the deceased's life rested in their coffin.

Attending funerals has had a great impact on my life. It has always reminded me to think about what I could offer to others, what service and legacy I could leave behind for society. The day that I leave this world, what will my report card look like? As an entrepreneur, besides pursuing extraordinary business performance and reaching high profit targets, what else can I contribute to society?

You will find that many successful enterprises are respected not only because they provide quality products and services that meet others' needs, they also actively contribute to society. In fact, respected companies love sharing the secrets of their success with others to help them learn, grow, and prosper. Furthermore, in the collective progress of companies, the wellbeing of society as a whole also improves, which I believe is the true social value of companies.

Over the years, I aimed to publish a book on the *Autopilot Leadership Model* that we had practiced for over ten years to share with others. I hope that this model does not only belong to our company, but also to society. Sharing my experiences and insights with others was the original intention of publishing this book.

The *Autopilot Leadership Model* originated from the idea of the *Invisible Leader* from the *Dao De Jing (道德經)*, which will be explained in Chapter 2. Combined with Western management methods, after more than ten years of brainstorming, exploring, learning, and implementing, we were finally able to refine and implement this system. You could say that this is the collective wisdom of our company.

In this model, people are the most important factor because both talent and teamwork are two very vital facets. Through the six elements of *Choosing the Right Talent, High Trust Environment, Highly Effective Team, Common Goal, Effective Empowerment,* and *Coaching and Developing Talent,* we aim to help our employees to unleash their full potential and achieve happiness. Moreover, we hope to attract even more talented people, and ensure business sustainability.

Over the past decade, the *Autopilot Leadership Model* has gone through rapid development and played an important role in our company, allowing me to become a relaxed and happy entrepreneur.

A few years ago, after I exchanged ideas with some friends about the *Autopilot Leadership Model,* they showed their deep interest and asked for the details of the model and asked why I had not written a detailed book about it. At the time, however, I felt that our model was not refined enough since we still had little practice and experience. The book was not ready to be published.

In early 2011, we thought about how we could celebrate the 20th anniversary of the company the following year. One colleague suggested publishing the *Autopilot Leadership Model* since we had fully adopted it and its results had been great thus far.

The theory of the *Autopilot Leadership Model* continued to mature and improve, and we gathered a lot of experience and case studies over the years. This consolidated book would let us further explore, practice, and optimize our system; making it more easily comprehensible and applicable so that others could learn from the insights that we would share in this text.

It was time to write the book!

We established an *Autopilot Leadership* Book Project Team to officially begin writing the book. It took around a year to collect data and conduct staff interviews. The team researched different case studies, held focus groups, prepared the first draft, and then amended it dozens of times. Finally, the group streamlined the 120,000 Chinese characters to about 60,000 characters. After repeated scrutiny, the team completed the full Chinese manuscript.

Before delivering the manuscript to the printing press, we invited employees from different departments to read over the draft, give their own evaluation and voice their opinions and suggestions. After the feedforward,[1] we conducted a final set of changes and completed the Chinese version of the book that is now in your hands in the English language. The process of writing and publishing reflected the above collective wisdom.

Here, I want to thank Mr. Lam Yu, Mr. Gary Huang, Ms. Sally Wang, Mr. Rockey Chen, Mr. Phoenix Li, Ms. Shen Jianping, Mr. Wu Dianzhao, and other employees for their incredible contribution and efforts in planning, creating, preparing, revising, and publishing the Chinese version.

To break through the language barrier, we decided to work on an English translation of our *Autopilot Leadership Model*. We hope that this new version will help us spread the combined wisdom of Eastern philosophies and methods of Western leadership to the global community beyond the initial reach of our Chinese version. The purpose of our publication is to introduce the core ideals of our leadership model, which we will follow up in the future with more books on the process of successful implementation and the story of our struggles and achievements.

I would like to express my gratitude to Mr. Steven Lau, Ms. Ida Wong, Ms. Winnie Yang, Ms. Anna Tung, Ms. Regina Lai and my daughter Jamie Lee for the production of the English version.

Thanks to the executive editor of Forbes China, for professional advice, ideas, and recommendations throughout the entire writing and publishing process Mr. Kang Jian.

I would like to thank our company's core management team and everyone who was involved in giving feedforward. Their valuable suggestions facilitated this book to become more refined and perfected.

I thank all the staff, partners, and colleagues who have served the company so well throughout the years. They have actively promoted, practiced, and participated in improving the *Autopilot Leadership Model* and have filled this book with rich case studies and stories.

Thanks to those friends who have encouraged me, along with the McGraw-Hill Education. They all have provided affirmation, support, and endorsement of the *Autopilot Leadership Model*, allowing us to confidently share our valuable experiences with you.

Of course, I would also like to thank my father Mr. Lee Man Tat, my mother Mrs. Lee Choi May Ling, my siblings, my wife and my two daughters. Without their support, care, and help, the company and I would not have made it today. I would never have had the platform and the opportunity to create the *Autopilot Leadership Model* nor the motivation to realize my dreams.

There are many more people I would love to show my gratitude toward, but am unable to do so in these few pages. I believe that this book, the hard work put into it, and the message behind it collectively embody the sincere appreciation and thankfulness of my colleagues and myself.

Today, the official publication of this book is a major milestone for us. It has created an introductory blueprint of the *Autopilot*

Leadership Model to help inspire others to learn from and try out this form of leadership. This model has not only helped us progress over the past decade, but I believe it will also continue to help our company grow far into the future by gradually realizing its full impact.

If this book and this model could be of inspiration to businesses and entrepreneurs, this would be our greatest source of recognition and encouragement.

The *Autopilot Leadership Model* still has room for improvement and there are more aspects to explore. I sincerely hope that readers can provide us with valuable comments and suggestions to further our cause.

Sammy Lee
June 2016

Endnote

1. Lang, Charlie. "Value seen in appraisals that are forward looking." *South China Morning Post*, May 19, 2007.

Preface

In many people's minds, an entrepreneur has complete control over the life and death of a business while facing the risks and pressures within its business development process.

Entrepreneurs are constantly unavailable; their time is committed to meetings and unending to-do lists. They manage an extremely hectic schedule while struggling to maintain a work-life balance; their mental and physical health, along with their relationships, deteriorates over time. Their schedule is defined by work, twenty-four seven.

I have discovered the key to overturning this stereotype—the *Autopilot Leadership Model*. In striving to become more of an *Invisible Leader*, I have been able to find leisure time to play sports, travel, brainstorm new strategies, and do what I like to do. Surprisingly, with the implementation of this model, I played my best game of golf, scoring 71 points, and won a club championship. "Work hard, play hard" has always been an important motto for me.

Some people may ask: Does such a hands-off CEO affect the management of their company? In fact, our company stayed on course and everything ran relatively smoothly because of this working style. In the past ten consecutive years, our company has achieved outstanding growth and has won the awards of "Best Employer in China" and "Best Employer in Asia."

Table of Contents

PART I

The Joy in Achieving
Autopilot Leadership

The Best Employer with a Golfer's Best Score of 71

A passionate golfer would understand that there is no easy way to reach a best score of 71 in this exciting sport. It requires serious dedication, continuous practice, perseverance, and gradual progress to eventually achieve a low handicap score. A game of golf usually takes around four hours to complete; I play around two to three games a week, and have been known to spend 12 consecutive days on the golf course.

Many entrepreneurs find themselves stuck in a no-win situation: they find it difficult to run a successful business without sacrificing their own interests and hobbies. How does

an entrepreneur who plays so much golf allocate enough time to run a growing business? It is already hard enough to become a qualified entrepreneur, so how does an avid golfer become a "Best Employer?"

I am happy to tell you that this lose-lose situation may not always be the case. While I enjoy pursuing my personal hobbies, my business has been running smoothly and promisingly as well. With due modesty, I hope I can remain a Best Employer with a golfer's best score of 71.

Golfing is a personal passion of mine. I appreciate the greenery of the natural environment, fresh air, the exhilaration from holing a shot, and the stress alleviation from the entire process. Because of this I enjoy playing golf with anyone, be it a business partner, a family council member, a board member, a fellow staff member, my wife, or even just by myself.

Besides golf, I have various other hobbies. I love snowboarding and often travel to colder countries like Canada to chase the slopes. I indulge in watching soccer and went overseas to see the 2002 Korean World Cup's third week matches, the 2006 German World Cup, and the 2014 Brazilian

World Cup competitions. I once traveled to Germany to attend a CEO conference, and while other CEOs spent their free time managing their businesses rigorously, I opted to watch the FIFA games instead.

Every year, I go on vacations with my family. I like to travel around the world with my wife and two daughters and enjoy each other's company. I am extremely lucky to be not only a very happy man, but also a healthy one because of the joy brought by my favorite hobbies, work, sports, and other aspects of life.

Our corporation promotes the *Three Balances of Life— Health, Family, and Work*. During a management meeting with 50 other employees, we conducted an evaluation of each person's performance in achieving the *Three Balances of Life*. Out of a maximum score of 10, I received a commendable 9.3. I hope to set my life as an example for others, to encourage them to strive for the same balance that can make our lives so much better.

For me, health is the pillar of strength in leading a happy life. Without the *Three Balances of Life*, the full possibilities of life would never be realized. Family is the home for our hearts; without a strong family, no matter how successful you are in other aspects of life your heart may still feel empty. Without a healthy body and a happy family, it is near impossible to maximize the contentment and happiness of life.

I can proclaim myself as being a content and fortunate entrepreneur only because I have found a balance between health, family, and work. I hope that my experience will motivate my employees and others to find their *Three Balances of Life*.

Now, you must be thinking: What is his secret?

Chapter 1

Happiness Stems from
Autopilot Leadership

Introduction

Perhaps you have already guessed: our secret must be the effective management and high productivity of our employees as they have successfully sustained the business while handling the piles of work and stress.

This is true: we own a passionate business with highly engaged employees, and cooperative and efficient teams. We have committed and responsible employees who collectively help the business a lot.

While our employees perform extraordinarily well at work, they also have time to pursue their own hobbies such as reading, learning, studying for a degree, playing sports, fishing, taking photographs, hiking, traveling, or recording their own album. In addition, they also spend a lot of time taking care of their families and enjoying their own personal leisure time. Although there are still some who have not yet achieved a good balance of the three components, you can also see their enthusiasm for work, their smiles, their confidence, and their passion for our business and for life.

Why has my happiness and energy for life spread around to the rest of my employees? Why is my contentment and success contagious to others around me?

In fact, my employees and I were not always this gratified and it took a long journey for us to discover how we could flip our frowns into smiles.

I used to have a very hectic schedule, constantly traveling back and forth between Hong Kong and Guangzhou, working overtime—sometimes 20 hours a day. The piles of documents created mountains on my desk and the phone never stopped ringing. There were many problems awaiting solutions.

Those frantic days took a major toll on my health and I developed hypertension, high cholesterol, fatty liver, and gout. My hair started to fall out. I still remember one afternoon when I felt an uncomfortable sensation in my chest and suspected that I had a heart condition. When I went to the hospital for a coronary angiogram, the doctor told me that even though the condition of my heart didn't cause major concern that time, it could become one in a decade's time if I carried on with my hectic lifestyle. My heart was heavy and I felt a pang of fear.

But that is all history now.

Fast forward to the present: I no longer have to micromanage the daily operations of the company and can completely rely on the capabilities of my core management team. Our employees no longer need close management and supervision to continue daily operations productively.

I never have to pick up the phone every ten minutes to discuss everyday operational issues. In fact, I have set my phone to permanent "call divert" mode or rely on secretarial services so that I can prioritize replying to the phone calls I have received. My main responsibilities concern the direction and strategy of our company, talent recruitment, and corporate culture. For three days every quarter, I hold a conference with the core management team. In addition, during monthly meetings, my core management team discusses the daily governance systems and other pressing issues among themselves, allowing each member to openly express their opinions for deliberation.

With these efficiently coordinated responsibilities, I still have enough time to participate in board meetings and family council meetings, as well as to regularly attend the company's important assemblies, including the strategic review and management meetings.

Another big change that complemented our company's progress was the improvement of my health as I spared more time to spend with my family, striking a better *Three Balances of Life—Health, Family, and Work.*

From then on, the company has launched onto a secure development track, with business performance reaching double-digit growth rates over the past ten consecutive years. Infinitus' brand value reached RMB36.889 billion or US$5.992 billion in 2014, ranking 46th in China's 500 Most Valuable Brands, a prestigious award presented by World Brand Lab.[1] In just 20 years, Infinitus' business has spread all over China and overseas. From 2000 to 2015, the company had grown more than 180 times.

From 2005–2016, the world's renowned human resources consulting firm Aon Hewitt has named our company as "Best Employer in China" (four times, among which we have just obtained the latest award in June 2016) and "Best Employer in Asia" (two times).[2] The two honors consider the four key criteria of high employee engagement, effective leadership, compelling employer brand, and high performance culture when evaluating companies over a nine-month span. In 2011, for the third time, Fortune China recognized us as "Best Company to Work for in China."[3] In 2016, we were named among the best companies to work for in Asia by *HR Asia Magazine*.[4] We were also certified by the Top Employers Institute as a Top Employer China 2016.[5] These are awards that acknowledge how a healthy work environment can become a firm's advantage in the marketplace. Attracting and retaining qualified personnel and nurturing a thriving corporate culture are just some elements that make up great working surroundings.

What was it that led to our major leap in progress?

It was not an influential person or a powerful book that motivated the evolution required to help me become a happy entrepreneur and a recognized "Best Employer." In fact, it was an exceptional leadership ideal—the *Autopilot Leadership Model*.

The autopilot mode of an airplane was designed to allow the pilot to focus on the major direction and routing of the aircraft instead of minding mechanical details. Much like the way all the minor gears are automatically controlled in this mode, the *Autopilot Leadership Model* was developed to enable a business leader to concentrate on the course of the enterprise rather than to mull over every detail personally.

Even without my physical presence in the company, everyone still efficiently carries out their duties and coordinates with others with the same objective. With minimal supervision, my employees instinctively and collectively activate their maximum productivity, pushing the company to perform better and progress quicker.

I will further discuss the details of the *Autopilot Leadership Model* in the second part of this book. In the meantime, let me talk about the advantages, the reasons, and the motivations for implementing the theory.

Let me kick off my explanation with the four reasons: *Happiness, Unleashing One's Potential, Attracting Talent,* and *Business Sustainability*.

Happiness

Happiness is a major buzzword in our company. It is an extremely subjective emotion that varies from person to person. We came up with a *Happiness Index* to measure the emotional wellbeing of our employees and to ensure they are enjoying the benefits of balancing between health, family, and work.

We always ask for everyone's *Happiness Index* during our meetings. In our circle of the meeting's participants, after the facilitator counts to three, everyone simultaneously holds out their happiness score with their fingers. The lowest number means the least happy and the highest means the most. Upon the unveiling, everyone takes turns to share the reasons behind their personal score.

If an employee's *Happiness Index* is less than six, it may hint at underlying problems. Hence, it is imperative that supervisors help their staff resolve specific problems to raise their overall index. Paying attention to employees' *Happiness Index* is equal to paying attention to their emotional health. We promote the *Autopilot Leadership Model* because helping our employees become happier is important to us.

There are many impressive enterprises that achieve tremendous success but only the leader is happy and their employees are not. We strive for success while we keep our employees' morale in mind. This outlook allows us to build a team of highly engaged employees. *Happiness* affects their passion, their performance, and the mechanics of the *Autopilot Leadership Model*, and consequently the company's wellbeing.

We hope that *Happiness* is not merely a buzzword, but a state of being for all of our employees. For example, when a supervisor delegates work, the supervisor should always consider the needs of their subordinates. Whether it is a parent-teacher conference or a family vacation or any other conflict with work schedules, supervisors and subordinates are highly encouraged to figure out the best way to utilize their full productivity. By allowing our employees the freedom to care about themselves, their family, and their health, they are able to lead the balanced lifestyle that is heavily advocated by our company.

As a testament to our high morale, many new employees have voiced their surprise as to how warm and understanding our company is. Some have even gone as far as to say that it almost feels like home. Compared with the social and industry average, our employee turnover rate is extremely low at 3 percent. As my employees are happy working at our company, I am equally proud and happy of their contentment and success.

When employees feel cared for, respected, and recognized, they in return have a deep sense of belonging, a strong willingness to work with us in the long run, and a mindset prepared to achieve greatness. The happiness of staff is reflected in the work they produce, creating greater value, and motivating further development and progress.

As one entrepreneur once said, "Take care of your employees—they will take care of your customers, and we will all receive greater returns."

Unleashing One's Potential

I remember when one of my employees shared one of his personal experiences.

He had only been working for us for six months. Unexpectedly, his supervisor assigned him to take charge of a large project, which included a multitude of components, a long working time horizon, and extremely high standards. More importantly, because he lacked in-depth experience and was still not entirely familiar with our operational style, he was not confident in completing this project. However, his supervisor said to him, "I have always admired the comprehensive way you tackle problems, and the ease with which you communicate with others. That is the reason why I consider you the best candidate to take on this project. Do not worry. Your colleagues and I will continuously support and stand by you. We believe that you can get it done."

With that in mind, this employee accepted the tremendous task. While he tackled this project, he encountered many problems and obstacles, but with everyone's help, he was able to successfully complete the project with flying colors. He commented, "I really did not believe that I would be able to finish all this work, but I did it in the end, surprising even myself."

Many of our employees have shared similar experiences of overcoming important challenges. By taking on something new, something unfamiliar, they were able to realize their true potential, to learn in the process, and to encourage themselves to push their boundaries. In fact, this is a major feature of our company and the reason why we have implemented the *Autopilot Leadership Model*.

Realizing employees' talents is not only a goal of our company but in fact a common mission among many modern enterprises. There are typically two ways to inspire employees to actualize their true talents. One way is to push, forcing them to complete a task regardless of how taxing it is, or else fire them or deduct wages as penalty for not fulfilling the task. With this style of management, employees will only burn out quickly. As they feel stressed and disrespected, they will not be inspired to reach their full abilities to accomplish anything. While it may produce very impressive results at times, it is nearly impossible to maintain that stressful mode of working. Employees will be extremely prone to feeling resentful and may even walk away.

Another way is the complete opposite of the previous, to pull. By creating a cooperative community, generating a productive atmosphere, and providing the right resources, employees will have a sense of trust from the company and its leadership. Although at times there may be obstacles and stress, employees will be able to develop a positive attitude and have the support behind them to persevere. Ultimately, it is possible that even the most seemingly impossible tasks can be outperformed.

The *Autopilot Leadership Model* utilizes the pulling governance style to stimulate and inspire employees to reach their full potential.

The prominent Hawthorne Experiment[6] in the study of management revealed the most important factors in inspiring employees. Rather than wage, position, or materialistic factors, in fact, recognition, respect, achievement, satisfaction, and other psychological factors proved to be even more vital.

What the *Autopilot Leadership Model* and the Hawthorne Experiment share is the emphasis on psychological factors— the importance of human relationships and emotions. They both see the significance of building a trusting relationship between leaders and subordinates so they can actively engage in listening to and effectively supporting one another. With these building blocks in place, you can begin to see a major shift in employee morale and an increase in productivity.

One employee told us from previous work experience in other firms that they had to follow strict guidelines and detailed step-by-step instructions that restricted their creativity and prevented them from discovering other effective means of completing tasks. Supervisors and employees had very rigid and controlled relationships, which created a tense working environment that was constantly in push enforcement mode. On the contrary, in our company, employees have greater scope to complete their duties using creative ways to enhance their productivity.

This staff member exclaimed, "The thing I prize the most from the *Autopilot Leadership Model* is the feeling of accomplishment. I can independently implement any plan of attack when given a specific task or goal, realize my hidden talents along the way, and grow from the experience."

I believe it is this sense of empowerment that makes the *Autopilot Leadership Model* so attractive and successful. It helps employees discover their true capabilities, raising productivity and personal value rather than causing stress from the fear of being reprimanded.

Attracting Talent

I always ask my staff, "Nowadays, do talented candidates choose companies, or do companies scout talent?" Many of them reply by saying that companies select talent, but I would like to think differently.

There are many applicants for jobs at Infinitus. However, in the end there are only a few of those who fit our company. On the other hand, we have to fight for this limited talent against the competition of other companies as well as their current employers. Because of this suitability reason, talented individuals pick companies and not the other way around.

Their criteria do not only involve salary and benefits, but also include company reputation, corporate culture, work environment, room for personal development, and overall happiness.

One of the reasons that we have implemented the *Autopilot Leadership Model* is to let our employees feel that they are valued. They have the capability to grow, so we hope that they are happy and willing to stay working with us.

As I have discussed in the previous sections, the *Autopilot Leadership Model* produces a happy and highly productive workplace to grow and to *Unleash One's Potential*, which is extremely attractive to even the most talented people.

Twice a year, we hold departmental team-building activities, funded by the company. Away from the office in the beautiful outdoors, these activities typically last two days, creating a healthy environment in which to share and exchange work experiences, play team-building games, get in touch with nature, and have a great time. The activities focus on being fun, engaging, and encouraging personal growth. Our company has implemented this popular event for over a decade now.

In addition, we also have recreational clubs, family fun days, book clubs, and a recreation area in our offices, all designed to make employees happy and a part of a healthy community. Moreover, we evaluate employees' salary schemes annually to ensure that the remuneration continues to be both competitive and attractive.

So far, the number of employees who have worked for the company for at least five years reached around 30 percent while our turnover rate is only 3 percent. This illustrates our ability to attract and retain qualified people to help grow our company.

"Employee Engagement" is a key component in selecting the "Best Employer". Our company scored an above average score of nearly 90 points in "Employee Engagement", higher by far compared to those of other participating companies.

In recent years, more and more of our employees began to share our corporate culture and our empowering management style with others around them and even some media reports picked up on our unique culture. In a snowball effect, more people gradually became interested in the work we do, and more people wanted to join our cause. While employees felt empowered by our company, our company was in fact empowered by them.

Progressively more effective implementation of the *Autopilot Leadership Model* creates the magnetic force necessary to attract the right type of talent. I believe that more competent talent will proactively choose our company, that these individuals will drive the company to achieve new heights, and that our company will continue to grow stronger.

Business Sustainability

As *Business Sustainability* is the ultimate goal and dream of entrepreneurs, it is also my dream for my company to be able to sustain progress indefinitely. However, a majority of enterprises only develop to a certain size as the entrepreneur's efforts, coaching and development, governance, and operational systems cannot keep up with the company's growth rate. These conditions result in shrinking market shares, declining profits, slower growth, and eventually bottlenecks. When management systems face this challenge, many fail to solve their issues, leading to a collapse.

This phenomenon is particularly prevalent in mainland China, where the average life expectancy of most enterprises is only three years. Businesses that survive for more than a decade are very rare, let alone those that survive for a century.

Over years of development, our company experienced many setbacks that prompted us to put our heads together to find ways of breaking out of the problem. We found that the solution to the bottleneck problem is to successfully implement a long-term effective business model. Regardless of the growth of earnings, the number of employees, or the volatile terrain of the market, this model must provide a company with the best tools to tackle any problems head-on.

Years of practice have proven why the *Autopilot Leadership Model* can break through these blockages, reverse the situation, and help the company to progress. Of course, what comes hand-in-hand with this model are mission, responsibility, and core values. Having a sense of mission is to believe that perseverance can go a long way in terms of results, profits, and goals so that enterprises can stand higher, see farther, and go further. Responsibility pushes companies to maximize their social value, gain public trust, respect, and support. Core values can provide the highest standards and guidelines for employees for work and life, to unite our community and raise morale.

For the past 20 years, our company has strived to improve these three areas, the details of which I will recount in later chapters. We have continued to promote and to implement the *Autopilot Leadership Model*, emphasizing the importance of mission, responsibility, and core values to find our edge compared with our competitors in the market, making new discoveries and breakthroughs, and creating a sustainable system to continue to grow our business.

Happiness, Unleashing One's Potential, Attracting Talent, and *Business Sustainability* are the reasons and the benefits of the *Autopilot Leadership Model.* You must be wondering what the origin of the *Autopilot Leadership Model* was and what the process of developing this model was like. Let me tell you the full story in detail.

Endnotes

1. "2014年《中国500最具价值品牌》排行榜—2014年(第十一届)世界品牌大会" *2014年《中国500最具价值品牌》排行榜—2014年(第十一届)世界品牌大会*. Web, April 25, 2016 at http://brand.icxo.com/brandmeeting/2014china500/brand42.htm.

2. "Aon Hewitt and LinkedIn Announce the Best Employers—China 2015 Awards." *News Releases*. Aon Plc, March 20, 2015. Web, May 16, 2016 at http://aon.mediaroom.com/Aon-Hewitt-and-LinkedIn-Announce-the-Best-Employers-China-2015-Awards.

3. "2007卓越雇主—中国最适宜工作的公司—Fortune China." *2007卓越雇主—中国最适宜工作的公司—Fortune China.* Fortune China, November 1, 2007. Web, August 7, 2014 at www.fortunechina.com/magazine/c/2007-11/01/content_2325.htm.

4. "21 Hong Kong Companies Named Best Companies To Work For In Asia" News Releases. *HR Asia*, May 3, 2016. Web, May 16, 2016 at http://hrasiamedia.com/21-hong-kong-companies-named-best-companies-to-work-for-in-asia.

5. "Certified Top Employers—Top Employers Institute" *Certified Top Employers—Top Employers Institute.* Web, May 16, 2016 at http://www.top-employers.com/Certified-Top-Employers/?Certificate=88.

6. Mayo, Elton. "Hawthorne Experiments" Web, April 25, 2016 at http://www.learnmanagement2.com/eltonmayo.htm.

Chapter 2

Becoming An
Invisible Leader

The Four Types of Leaders

In 1997 when I took part in an internal training course within the company, Lao Zi's (老子)[1] *Dao De Jing (道德經)*[2] was first brought to my attention. As stated by legends, renowned as a mystic keeper of the Imperial Court's archives around the sixth century B.C., Lao Zi (老子) was the founding father behind philosophical Daoism (道教).[3] Daoism (道教)

synthesizes metaphysics, nature, and ethics. This theory has its conception in the *Dao De Jing (道德經)*, written by Lao Zi (老子). Lao Zi's (老子) *Dao De Jing (道德經)* can be translated into *The Law (or Canon) of Virtue and its Way*. It circles around how "the Dao" (道) finds expression in "De" or "Virtue" (德). Particularly, the text highlights the importance of "Zi Ran" or "Naturalness" (自然) and "Wu Wei" or "Nonaction" (無為).[4] One concept that really struck me was that of the four different levels of leaders.

Quoted from the *Dao De Jing (道德經)*:

> 太上, 下知有之。其次, 親而譽之。
> 其次, 畏之。其次, 侮之。

An English translation by Sanderson Beck:

> The best leaders the people barely know.
> The next best they love and praise.
> The next they fear.
> And the next they hate.[5]

From my understanding, it means that the ultimate leader exists but remains invisible—they are called an *"Invisible Leader"*; the next best is a leader who is loved, called a "Natural Leader"; the next is a leader who is feared; and the worst type of leader is one who is hated.

When I first heard of this verse, I was immediately taken by the prospect of becoming an *Invisible Leader* because it was the perfect style of management that I had always been searching for.

Back then our company was going through a difficult period and I was always struggling with daily affairs to the point of exhaustion. Every time I traveled from Hong Kong back to Guangzhou for work, I would see the words "Unresolved

Issues" slashed across the chalkboard. Had I not physically been at the office to delegate all the work, all those items would have permanently remained on that board. Meetings usually lasted up until the late hours of the night and resumed extremely early in the morning and the difficult process would perpetually repeat itself.

I knew then that it was time for a change or else our management team would suffer disastrously from the company's expansion. So we faced the big question: How could we change the status quo for the better?

Lao Zi's (老子) concept of the *Invisible Leader* came to my mind at the very opportune moment when we were deeply in need of it.

In the current business world, a lot of leaders are measured by their presence in their company. But under the *Autopilot Leadership Model*, we advocate doing just the opposite. A company's performance should not rely on the quantity of the leader's presence and it should be able to run effectively through the model's various steps.

Traditionally, politicians and distinguished business leaders reached the second level of leadership, leaders who are loved, the Natural Leaders. Even the greatest ancient Chinese strategist Zhuge Liang (諸葛亮)[6] led the same way, concerning himself with all matters first hand. Although he received high praise for his tremendous work, according to Lao Zi's (老子) typology of leadership, Zhuge Liang (諸葛亮) never reached the highest status.

My dream was to beat the odds and reach that highest level, to become an *Invisible Leader* and also to pass on this leadership model to my fellow entrepreneurs.

Imagine a liberating working environment where employees have free time and very few meetings. Life would have its own natural rhythm, where we could pursue hobbies, and spend time with family while the business would advance simultaneously. When the *Three Balances of Life—Health, Family,* and *Work—* are established, the world can be a beautiful place.

We opened the door to a 2,500-year-old secret philosophized by Lao Zi (老子). By combining his theory with our practice, we began to explore, form, and perfect the *Autopilot Leadership Model.*

The *Inverted Triangle*

As I mentioned in the previous section, our company initially went through a difficult phase, where a strict hierarchy centralized the decision-making process. Every choice was passed down from the business leader for everyone else to implement. It was a slow managerial process that was inefficient and spurred customer dissatisfaction.

At that time, as opposed to our currently *Inverted Triangle,* our company's operational and decision-making structure paralleled an upright triangle with the highest level of management at the top, the following levels receding down the triangle until the front-line staff, and the customers were positioned last. As every call that needed to be made traveled down this pyramid, decision making was inefficiently prolonged.

The biggest paradox was that the top management ranks were furthest away from the customers and the market, yet they were responsible for making the big decisions. How could that make any sense when the front-line employees situated at the bottom of the upright triangle were really the ones who knew the market firsthand but were given no authority at all to help direct the company?

To get away from this predicament, we had to adopt a new creative management method, a leadership style that could utilize the market knowledge of the front-line staff to help solve our top management problems while I could lean back and practice becoming an *Invisible Leader*.

Thus, we decided to flip the upright triangle on its head to form an *Inverted Triangle* to restructure the company. The CEO would be at the bottom layer. Stacked on that level would be the top management ranks supporting the back office, which would serve the front-line staff that sat above their level. And ultimately, the customers would be at the top layer as our company became entirely customer-oriented. These were major changes. As the chief, I positioned myself to serve our staff, and our entire company was geared to serve our customers.

There was an article from Harvard University that narrated the relationship between a shepherd and his sheep. To tell a good shepherd from a bad one, you only need to look at the way he positions himself in relation to his flock. A bad shepherd stands in the front and leads his flock of sheep. He would have to spend a lot of time chasing after the ones that were left behind or ones that strayed from the flock. But a good shepherd merely follows his sheep, which would naturally find grass to graze on. He would only need to step in if a few of his sheep wandered too far from the rest. This article coined the term "Leading from Behind."[7]

In fact you can see the parallelism between Harvard's "Leading from Behind" and the concept of our *Inverted Triangle*—a successful leader gives their employees space to be creative and accomplish tasks by their own means and only steps in to guide and advise when their employees are in need.

In contention for Hewitt's "Best Employer in China" and "Best Employer in Asia" awards, we realized that there were a surprising number of hotel enterprises that also received the same award. Human resources experts suggest that because hospitality businesses are extremely customer-oriented, they dedicate a lot of time supporting their front-line staff. With an automatic response system, whenever customers have any questions, front-line employees are trusted and given the power to solve their problems independently without having to constantly ask for permission. As decisions are not required to pass through each level of management, problem solving becomes quick and easy.

The *Inverted Triangle* model is becoming more and more popular in the modern business world and it also became our first step toward adopting the *Autopilot Leadership Model*.

The frame of decision making takes into account the *Inverted Triangle* structure of the company. In 2003, to protect the vision of staff, the company decided to replace all the computer displays with LCD monitors. But whose monitors should be replaced first—those of top management or the other staff? We finally decided to replace the monitors of the employees who were responsible for entering sales orders. They are front-line staff, working extremely long hours at their computers. Following them were the staff at the branch companies because they directly serve customers. Then, the third wave of installments was for the headquarters staff, and finally managerial employees.

During my limited visits to the Guangzhou office, most of my time is dedicated to meeting the Core Management Team to guide the company's strategic direction. I always ask if there is anything I can help them with or if there is anything they want to consult on. I do not want to become a dictator who makes all the decisions no matter whether small or great. Rather, I want to be the source of support for our staff, the pillar for all the people who have made our company progress so far.

This *Inverted Triangle* mindset ultimately directs all our efforts towards our customers. Also, because of this customer-oriented emphasis, our company devised our own employee and customer satisfaction surveys to monitor the progress and to gather feedforward on areas for improvement.

In the beginning of 2000, we launched our first customer satisfaction survey and received a score of 60 out of a full score of 100. However, as we adopted the *Inverted Triangle* and the *Autopilot Leadership Model* in our management style, our score improved. Progressively, we reached a customer satisfaction score of 89 in 2013.

To successfully implement the *Inverted Triangle* model, managerial employees should stand back to support and trust their staff. Flipping the triangle may not be that difficult, but maintaining it proves extremely hard. Just a misstep or one wrong word from supervisors could reverse the triangle at any time. Therefore, to sustain the *Inverted Triangle* in its position, the key component is the *Power of Trust*, which is the following topic of this chapter.

The Power of Trust

Trust plays an important role in all of our lives.

For example, every morning, when we wash our faces, we never question if the water flowing from the tap is clean or not. When we drive and meet a green light, we never doubt whether we can cross an intersection safely or will crash. When we ride a plane, we never worry if the pilots are capable or not. A child will never question whether their parents love them or not.

This is the basic *Power of Trust* and also the building block of our society. Without trust, there would be no communication, exchange, cooperation, or love, friendship, and romance. Society would turn into chaos and there would be no order at all.

Some say that we are living in a low trust society. Can we still believe and rely on others? In my opinion, untrustworthy individuals only make up a minority and most people deserve our trust and our benefit of the doubt.

Francis Fukuyama wrote in *Trust: The Social Virtues and The Creation of Prosperity* that trusting relationships in China are heavily based on blood relations.[8] This deems outsiders of the family as untrustworthy and forcefully creates a society with very little trust. Employers do not trust their employees and vice versa. The key to breaking through this weakness among many Chinese family enterprises is for the owner to establish trusting relationships beyond family ties.

In the business world, trust is equally important. Imagine a CEO had to make all the decisions rather than trust in the capability of their employees or allow employees to work but send a supervisor for constant monitoring, with every detail put into question. How could it be possible for that company to make any progress at all?

Management research experts suggest that an environment of distrust creates a need for extra supervision, effort, and resources to make things work. Employees are swamped with piles of work and meetings, which do not create any added value. Stress increases, morale decreases, mutual complaints arise, and an overwhelming sense of discontentment floods the business. An unhappy employee will bring that negative energy to their work. This contagious discontent will reveal itself to customers, which will in turn affect the reputation of the company. Ultimately, this jeopardizes overall business performance.

So in order to satisfy customers, employees should be catered to first by creating a trusting environment. They must foster a community that recognizes, encourages, and respects all employees to utilize their full talent. Under this model, employers do not need to concern themselves with every little detail of their business and can delegate work accordingly to their employees. Employees can automatically complete their duties without supervision all the time.

Trust is a powerful force in creating strong bonds between employers and employees. By respecting, recognizing, and caring for employees, this environment will encourage employees to do their best. I reckon that trust is the main building block for the *Autopilot Leadership Model* and a key prerequisite for becoming an *Invisible Leader*.

Endnotes

1. Ames, Roger T. "Laozi (Chinese Daoist Philosopher)." *Encyclopedia Britannica.* Encyclopedia Britannica, May 12, 2014. Web, August 7, 2014 at global.britannica.com/EBchecked/topic/330163/Laozi.
2. "Daodejing (Chinese Literature)." *Encyclopedia Britannica.* Encyclopedia Britannica, May 17, 2013. Web, August 7, 2014 at global.britannica.com/EBchecked/topic/582950/Daodejing.
3. Strickmann, Michel. "Daoism (Chinese Philosophy and Religion)." *Encyclopedia Britannica.* Encyclopedia Britannica, February 9, 2014. Web, August 7, 2014 at global.britannica.com/ EBchecked/topic/582972/Daoism.
4. Strickmann, Michel. "Daoism (Chinese Philosophy and Religion)." *Encyclopedia Britannica.* Encyclopedia Britannica, February 9, 2014. Web, August 7, 2014 at global.britannica.com/ EBchecked/topic/582972/Daoism.
5. Beck, Sanderson. "Dao De Jing: Way Power Book." *Wisdom Bible.* May 1, 2002. Web, September 19, 2014 at www.san.beck .org/Laotzu.html#17.
6. "Zhuge Liang (Chinese Adviser)." *Encyclopedia Britannica.* Encyclopedia Britannica, August 3, 2012. Web, August 7, 2014 at global.britannica.com/EBchecked/topic/116615/Zhuge-Liang.
7. Hill, Linda A. "Leading from Behind" *Harvard Business Review.* May 5, 2010. Web, Apr 25, 2016. at https://hbr.org/2010/05/ leading-from-behind.
8. Fukuyama, Francis. *Trust: The Social Virtues and The Creation of Prosperity.* Free Press, 1996.

Chapter 3

How was the *Autopilot Leadership Model* Found?

Introduction

I was deeply captured by the *Invisible Leader* mentioned by Lao Zi (老子) in his *Dao De Jing (道德經)*. Yet, Lao Zi (老子) never disclosed the steps in becoming an *Invisible Leader*. Without a system, how could we reach this level of leadership? We began to think, to explore, to learn, and to practice.

During a business trip in 2000, I found a book written by Larry Reynolds called *The Trust Effect: Creating the High Trust High Performance Organization.*[1] The author is a well-known management expert. In this book, he focuses on the importance of trust to the development and progress of an organization and produces concrete steps and methods to build such an enterprise. It was published in simplified Chinese in 2006 and I had the honor of writing a recommendation for its publication.

I treasured this book because the tremendous transformation that stemmed from trust that was described in this book inspired me to follow its blueprint. Moreover, the steps and methods it included were invaluable to this trust-building process.

In 2000, this text had not yet been published in Chinese. Therefore I asked a few colleagues to translate it section by section into Chinese for the managers' reference. Some read the Chinese version, some read the English, and everyone had their own understanding of the text. After around six months of learning and sharing with each other, everyone digested the vital concept that trust is imperative in creating a successful and effective organization. While we applied this notion to our own company, we further realized the gains from achieving this high-trust environment through using effective methods, like OPERA, which is a management tool for Effective Empowerment that we will discuss in Chapter 8.

In 2002, we also found a book by the name of *The Five Dysfunctions of a Team*[2] by Patrick Lencioni, which talks about how to overcome the lack of trust in a team through background sharing. Thus, we tried using this method to bolster trust in our offices.

We often host background-sharing sessions offsite. One of the most memorable sessions was in a hot spring. In a comfortable environment with my management team, I first recounted my childhood, my work experience, hobbies, obstacles, unforgettable moments, highs and lows, and things I had always kept to myself. I candidly revealed everything there was to know about me to set myself as an example. With that introduction, everyone else began to share the stories and no one wanted the session to end. We stayed there for almost three hours until our skin turned white. It was the longest I had ever been in a hot spring.

Through that experience, our management team immediately found ourselves closer to each other than ever. Our exchanges and communication were much more effective and our entire management team progressively overcame the barriers that prevented building a high-trust group. We felt that this method was extremely compelling in bringing positive change to our group and decided to promote this program throughout all departments and levels of the company.

After a period of practice, we found that trust is the prerequisite to building a high-trust organization. After heavy deliberation, we decided to name *High Trust Environment* as one of our core elements of the *Autopilot Leadership Model*.

In 2000, our company hit rock bottom. Everyone was skeptical about whether we could turn our situation around and lacked faith in our business. To raise morale, we promoted the theme of "New Era, New Mission, New Glory."

In 2001, we introduced the first five-year-plan with three focuses: the China Market, Traditional Chinese Medicine, and the Infinitus Business. On the surface it may seem as if we are keeping our to-do-list at the bare minimum, but in reality, it has helped us focus on the three major areas instead of being distracted by other issues. By consolidating our resources, we achieved great results. Our performance flew off the charts, and these changes turned our adversity into an opportunity, creating a new flourishing era.

From 2000 to 2001, although we focused on a certain targeted few to improve on, the results of our development were unexpectedly phenomenal. After further analysis and reflection, we realized that it was because everyone had a clear

Common Goal, which united everyone. With unified hearts and actions, everyone acted consistently with their words, sparking passion, commitment, and cooperation. The collective synergy created great performance results.

During this process, we found that *Common Goal* was another important element for the *Autopilot Leadership Model*. Similar to the way we found this content, others followed in the same footsteps through theory, practice, and refinement.

In December 2002, we held a management meeting with senior executives in Hainan. Throughout two full days, we talked through the strengths and weaknesses, the successes and failures of our experiences. We also summarized the theory, logic, content, and reasons for structuring and defining the *Autopilot Leadership Model*. After the meeting, we introduced the first complete version of the blueprint for the following *Autopilot Leadership Model* with its four mindsets, five reasons, and six elements.

Previous Version of the *Autopilot Leadership* Model

Four mindsets:
- Patience
- Firmness
- Tolerance
- Si Li Ji Ren(思利及人) or Consider Collective Benefits Before Acting

Five reasons:
- Business Sustainability
- Unleashing One's Potential

- Happiness
- Snowball Effect
- Attracting Talent

Six elements:
- Choosing the Right Talent
- High Trust Environment
- Highly Effective Team
- Common Goal
- Effective Empowerment
- Coaching and Developing Talent

However, we recognized that a good leadership model should be simple and commonly understood. After seven years of practice and promotion, we found that the initial four mindsets, five reasons, and six elements sometimes overlapped and caused confusion and difficulty in implementation. Thus, in 2009, the core management team and I spent two days fixing the problems of the *Autopilot Leadership Model* through in-depth discussions. Through this process we finally streamlined our design and proposed our current version with four reasons and six elements.

During this undertaking, perhaps you have already realized the depth and variety of resources we utilized to absorb information and eventually turn it into implementable wisdom. From trial and error, reflection, concept, and perseverance, we continuously revised and refined our practice. In this way, we explored our boundaries step by step, pushed our frontiers, and gradually became stronger and wiser as well. The achievement and the journey are both things to cherish and learn from.

Today, we share this book on the *Autopilot Leadership Model* to dive deeper into its mechanics, its origins, and its experiences. Hopefully you will have your own reflections from reading it. We welcome your questions, challenges, or any comments for our feedforward bank. I sincerely hope that we can use your help to continue to perfect our theory and practice. We hope that the *Autopilot Leadership Model* can take off and achieve its full value.

Endnotes

1. Reynolds, Larry. *The Trust Effect: Creating the High Trust High Performance Organization.* Nicholas Brealey Publishing, 1997.
2. Lencioni, Patrick. *The Five Dysfunctions of a Team.* Jossey-Bass, 2002.

PART II

What is *Autopilot Leadership*?

The Six Elements of the
Autopilot Leadership Model

- Choosing the Right Talent
- High Trust Environment
- Highly Effective Team
- Common Goal
- Effective Empowerment
- Coaching and Developing Talent

As mentioned in Chapter 3, Lao Zi's (老子) concept of the *Invisible Leader* in the *Dao De Jing (道德經)* was the earliest inspiration for the founding of the *Autopilot Leadership Model*. This unique model embodies historical and modern philosophies to guide organizations on how to run smoothly and effectively.

Many questions arise when we mention *Autopilot Leadership*. What kind of model is it? How can an organization be self-operational? How can a firm optimize performance, employee satisfaction, growth, and development?

Whenever I share this model with others, I also emphasize that it is a "leadership model" rather than a "management model." Harvard Business School's Professor John Kotter once said, "Management provides control and solves problems. Leadership provides motivation."[1] I strongly agree with this view. In my opinion, "management" focuses on supervision, control, and the present. It relies on rules and regulations, requires playing by the rulebook, and focuses on operational management. By contrast, "leadership" focuses on leading a team to a future collective destination, training others to trust and rely on the strength of their team, and encouraging responsive change and innovation. It inspires others to break through and improve the status quo. It unlocks unique talents and strengths to maximize productivity.

Under the traditional management model, all the responsibilities of making major decisions on a company's direction and development fell solely on the leader. This concentration of power is largely top-down and heavily result-oriented, which neglects the initiative and creativity of employees. Much like robots, employees simply follow directions and execute their narrowly-defined tasks. With this method, the significance of the process is diminished substantially.

On the contrary, the *Autopilot Leadership Model* relies on people's capabilities with the prerequisite of strategy formulation, goal setting, and proper talent recruitment. With respect, encouragement, and motivation, employees will be inspired to do their best and unleash their hidden abilities. At the same time, leaders can focus on personal development and

building a strong team. This will allow employees to push their boundaries and create synergy among team members to act as a powerful force in reaching more challenging goals.

Thus, the cornerstones of the *Autopilot Leadership Model* are *Talent* and *Team*. These two concepts are interdependent as they complement each other. Talent is the foundation of a *Highly Effective Team* and a *High Trust Environment* is the soil in which people can be nurtured. In addition, high levels of trust and efficiency can unlock the secrets to higher achievement and progress.

Why have we chosen to position *Choosing the Right Talent* as the first element of our model? Because a corporation's productivity and achievements depend on the employees it recruits. Without these accomplished individuals, a company will not be able to perform at its best. Without the right people, challenging goals can only be imagined and not realized.

One important point to acknowledge, however, is that there are no perfect people but there are perfect teams. Only a team can overcome the limits of a single person through synergy and complementing strengths. Trust, however, is the mandatory foundation for creating a successful organization. Within a *High Trust Work Environment*, members of a *Highly Effective Team* are free to leverage on others' strengths, produce incredible results, and find an edge over their competition.

The next step is to find a direction and set a goal, which leads to another element on our list—*Common Goal*. By establishing a shared objective, every member of the team can strive towards the same direction. Through *Effective Empowerment*, employees will have clearly defined roles and responsibilities. This will inspire them to utilize their unique strengths, combining everyone's gifts to achieve their collective objective.

Last but not least, *Coaching and Developing Talent* creates a powerful domino effect, pushing all six elements forward. This crucial step extensively educates the entire company about the *Autopilot Leadership Model* from top to bottom. It also promotes employees to develop their skills and grow as

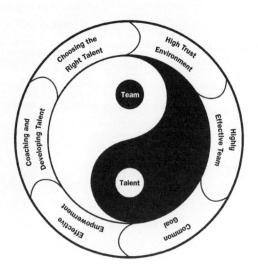

team players to meet the higher requirements of a progressive company in order to attain business sustainability.

From *Choosing the Right Talent* to *Coaching and Developing Talent*, the six elements of the *Autopilot Leadership Model* create a dynamic loop. The model persistently utilizes talent and teams to improve and satisfy many needs of the enterprise. Through continuous practice, an organization can optimize business performance, employee satisfaction, growth, and business sustainability. All of the above are stepping-stones for a business leader to pursue the peak state of leadership—becoming an *Invisible Leader*.

Endnote

---

1. Kotter, John P. "What Leaders Really Do." *Harvard Business Review.* December 2001. Web, August 20, 2014 at www.keele.ac.uk/media/keeleuniversity/fachealth/cml/ what_leaders_really_do.pdf.

Chapter 4

Choosing the Right Talent

Choosing the Right Talent

- Cultural Fit > Capability
- Position People Properly
- Dare to Employ People More Competent than You
- Competency Model

Even if a company has a first-class strategy and first-class products, without a first-class team of employees it will not be able to accomplish anything. Although there are many accomplished candidates in the working world today, companies often find it difficult to hire competent talent who match with their corporate culture as other enterprises are also competing for the same people.

Without the right talent, strong teamwork, or synchronization with the company's corporate culture, even with the best aspirations a company could perform badly. On the other hand, an organization with the right resources and a *Highly Effective Team* can attract more suitable employees and boost a company from good to great.

Traditional standards of appointing personnel have heavily emphasized capability. Yet, we focus more on how our people fit with our corporate culture. In addition, we heavily highlight the importance of *Positioning People Properly* to boost work effectiveness. Also, we encourage our employees to *Dare to Employ People More Competent than They* so as to raise overall proficiency. To conclude this chapter, I will share our company's *Competency Model* to explore the issues of *Choosing the Right Talent* to help our company's talent pool grow.

Cultural Fit > Capability

In hiring employees, we emphasize *Cultural Fit > Capability*. While *Capability* refers to knowledge, qualifications, or diplomas, *Cultural Fit* refers to character, attitude, values, and a person's suitability for a company's corporate culture. In our company, *Cultural Fit* overrides professional competence. This does not mean that we completely neglect concrete skills, but we require that our employees fit into our organization's customs. *Capability* can be easily improved, but *Cultural Fit* is hard to find. Corporate culture is the solidified and everlasting soul of a company that affects every step of its development.

If team members' values are consistent with each other's, it helps avoid unnecessary conflicts and encourages enjoyable cooperation. If everyone has their own separate values and ways of doing things, this team would doubtfully achieve their *Common Goal*. Improvement can be made in terms of skills; yet it is difficult to change a person's values. Therefore, their incompatibility with the company's culture could jeopardize the entire organization.

In our opinion, *Cultural Fit* is more important than *Capability*. We have no way of working with someone who is highly capable but is the antithesis of what our company stands for. Even if this person is a genius, there can be no successful partnership. Conversely, we like to accept individuals who agree with our corporate culture even if they lack certain skills.

However, in our company we do not advocate dismissing employees easily. Only when they demonstrate an integrity problem would we take decisive measures in letting them go. Regardless of seniority, if an employee shows strong *Capability* but is extremely unwilling to cooperate with their colleagues or when they place their personal interests above the team, then we will ask the employee to leave.

More and more enterprises are beginning to evaluate their employees' values, but different companies have different approaches for aligning corporate culture with their employees' values.

In our company, *Cultural Fit* is not only considered when evaluating employees at the manager level. Rather, we evaluate a mandatory weight of 20 percent of employees' performance appraisals in terms of how they promote and practice our corporate culture. We have adopted an annual Employee Satisfaction Survey to assess management's contribution to our corporate culture. An example would be the quantity and quality of supervisors actively engaging and counseling their subordinates. This survey allows our employees to know that we take our core values seriously, to raise their awareness, and to strengthen their embodiment of it in their everyday behavior.

If you have ever eaten spicy hot pot, you know that this cuisine relies on its incredible flavors and spices. Whatever is dipped into the pot is retrieved spicier. After consumption for a while, additional broth is required. If the extra broth is bland, it will dilute the entire pot's flavor; but you can maintain the hot pot's seasoned flavor if you add spicy broth.

In essence, a company's culture is like spicy hot pot. If its corporate culture is spicy enough, whoever is inducted into the company will adopt its spiciness. Every employee's values and attitudes will absorb the company's common ideals. Yet, it is important to add the right talent, the spicy broth, to our mix to avoid corporate culture dilution.

For the new hires, we are not eager to push them to produce immediate results. Instead we first induct them through our orientation, educate them about our corporate culture, and integrate them into our team with background-sharing and team-building activities. This will allow our new employees to become a flavorful part of our hot pot of talent.

Many CEOs would argue: "Although *Cultural Fit* is very important, when hiring new employees shouldn't we select candidates based on technical *Capability* first and worry about *Cultural Fit* later?" In my opinion, I would rather slow down progress to sift out the right employees instead of hiring people who do not match up with our corporate culture at all. Hiring one unsuited individual could have a multitude of negative consequences and would eventually affect the overall performance of the team and the entire organization. Should that individual produce inappropriate results, unnecessary resources would be needed to resolve those issues.

Position People Properly

Another aspect of our element of *Choosing the Right Talent* is *Positioning People Properly*. After hiring the suitable employees, we need to evaluate their character, abilities, and expertise to fully utilize their productive talents. By utilizing a comprehensive assessment to understand the ideal position for them, we can realize their strengths and reap the maximum value of their work.

Modern enterprises now have very meticulous divisions of work, where each position requires specific qualifications. Because everyone has their unique expertise and strengths, it is only necessary that we position an individual in the most suitable post. If successfully accomplished, this can inspire enthusiasm, creativity, and perpetual hunger for learning. For example, if we place an employee who is full of innovative ideas but is weak in quantitative analysis in a postproduction and number-crunching position, they may not be able to perform to the best of their abilities. Consequently, they will lack a sense of accomplishment and will feel discouraged about their work.

Therefore, only when employees are placed in the right position will they actualize their full potential and maximize their value to the company. Not only will this make subordinates happier, but it will also confirm the effectiveness of the leaders' empowerment. On the contrary, if employees are misplaced, they will become dissatisfied, making them prone to mistakes and producing flawed work, which will eventually force them to leave.

Positioning People Properly has two different aspects— understanding an individual's character and delegating appropriately. First, one must be able to fully understand a candidate's strengths, weaknesses, abilities, and passions. Secondly, the company should assign the candidate to the right post that matches their aptitude and interests.

We can use employees' personal information to understand their work experience, educational background, expertise, and more. In addition, through *Competency Models* or working style surveys, we can use a more scientific approach to fully comprehend and merge employees' aptitudes with suitable jobs. Through different projects or rotational programs, perhaps we can better understand each employee's strengths and find their right fit in the company. Active participation in different projects and positions can build a more all-rounded experience for our employees. At the same time, it gives us a comprehensive report of their performance and expertise.

In addition to team-building activities like background-sharing, new employees' self-introductions is another way to get to know our employees. During orientation or the first meeting they join, we encourage new hires to share their academic background, work experience, hobbies, and other topics. With back- and forth-exchanges, questions, and other activities, old and new employees not only get to know each other better, but also build a solid foundation for teamwork.

Our company also promotes rotational programs or project assignments for new employees to test their capabilities. We allow our employees to gain a more diversified working experience as they are exposed to different projects. They can expand their work portfolio, work with a multitude of distinct personalities, and establish overall good working relationships between departments for the future. Simultaneously, this is an opportunity for them to shine and for their supervisors to find fitting roles for them within the company.

Furthermore, we encourage heightened group communication between employees to discuss each person's strengths, areas for improvement, ways to bolster cooperation, and career-planning options. The positioning and career development of an employee should never be determined by a single person in order to avoid subjectivity and impartiality.

We cannot always match the right people with the right jobs. It is important to recognize that mistakes are made through trial and error, and that practice makes perfect. We should always be more open to testing people and giving them more than just one chance.

At times when we realize that an employee may not be the best person for a specific post, we discourage letting them go right away. Rather, we encourage their supervisors to consider the reasons for the mismatches. For example, there may be instances when an employee possesses *Cultural Fit* but their expertise does not match the specific job requirements and the person cannot fully utilize their talents in that position. In those cases, we sit the employee down for a chat to analyze the reasons behind this mismatch. Subsequently, we look for new opportunities to help find a more suitable role for them. If that individual still cannot perform well even after the adjustment, we would then consider dismissal as a last resort.

Dare to Employ People More Competent than You

Our company commonly uses the Talent Selection Score as a basis for assessing the ability of a supervisor in *Choosing the Right Talent*. If a supervisor has a personal competency score of 90 but their subordinate only has 60, then that team's overall average score would be dragged down to 60 points. On the contrary, if the supervisor scores 80 points but the subordinate scores 90 or above, then the team's overall performance will receive a score of 90. Comparing the two scenarios, the latter holds the higher overall team score and the level of *Choosing the Right Talent* will be greatly strengthened.

A leader's true value does not lie solely on how strong their personal capabilities are. Instead, it relies heavily on their ability to appoint the right people and partner with others who are stronger than they are. A good leader should not be solely concerned with their individual report card and should focus more on the team's report card. Furthermore, it is the duty of a leader to be able to scout talented individuals who can surpass the leader's own capabilities to generate productive growth in the company and to learn more from their strengths.

There is a Chinese saying, "三人行必有我師焉," which means "when three people work together, there must be one who will have something to teach me."[1] Frequently, leaders do not employ others who are more competent than them in fear of losing their job by hiring a stronger subordinate. This situation would mirror the structure of the Russian Matryoshka dolls, where each level of employees is weaker than the last, where the front-line employees become the weakest link in the whole organization. This could severely compromise the team and even the entire company.

At times, when a leader exercises strong control over their subordinates, they could act as a lid that suppresses the abilities of the team. Employees would find it extremely difficult to demonstrate their skills. Moreover, the level of its independent leader would cap the overall productivity of the team. In that case, the leader would become the obstacle to collective development. Only leaders who dare to trust in employing people who are more competent than they are can then uncover the lid and open up a wider world and truly realize the potential for advancement.

In fact, the capabilities of a leader and their staff are entirely related. There is no absolute comparison between the two. Perhaps in one respect, the subordinates are relatively stronger in terms of concrete skills, or even the overall capabilities of the subordinates are on par with the leader. If a leader can confidently employ people who are more competent, they will be able to widen their own horizons, persistently learn from others, and find the true value behind delegating and working within a team.

In reality, there is no such thing as a perfect person who is stronger than everyone else. There should be no competition between leaders and their subordinates in terms of competence. Instead they should build a strong sense of synergy within this partnership. The focus should be placed on collective contribution and performance. Only leaders who can appoint and utilize more capable individuals can push the entire organization to new heights.

If a leader dares to take on this challenge and trust in the ability of their staff, then they can concentrate on the big picture issues instead of wasting time worrying about every detail.

Competency Model

You may ask, "How can we objectively and systematically assess a person?"

The *Competency Model* we have developed measures the quality of talent in our pool of employees so that we can recruit talented people more practically.

In 2005, our company entered a new stage of rapid development, in which the demand for people skyrocketed. This got us thinking: What are our guidelines for *Choosing the Right Talent*? How should we define talent? How can we teach every leader in our company to select the right employees and delegate work appropriately? With these questions in mind, we decided to introduce the *Competency Model* to increase the effectiveness of hiring new personnel.

How did we do it? The simplest approach was to directly adopt the common competency models that other enterprises had been using as a starting point. This approach was simple and convenient; however, it did not align with our unique corporate culture.

Consequently, we took a long time to develop our own internal set of aptitude standards through conducting different focus groups, highlighting particular important characteristics, research and analysis, with integration of our corporate culture.

Elements of the *Competency Model*:

- We > I
- Breakthroughs and Innovation
- Pragmatism and Integrity
- Customer-oriented

For each of these topics, we defined a detailed list of behavioral indicators that would help clearly identify and quantify the quality of the staff.

In 2006, we officially launched the *Competency Model* for employees of the manager level and above for their performance appraisal. Although we limited its application to the manager grade and above, we could see already the major advantages and changes it brought to our company. This guided everyone into evaluating their own work and seeing their areas for improvement.

After a period of implementation, we found that some of the model's contents were not easy to understand and not applicable in practice. Although the overall model made our recruitment process more effective, we recognize that there are still certain inadequacies that we need to address. For all intents and purposes, this *Competency Model* is still a work in progress.

Despite the Eastern origins of the *Autopilot Leadership Model*, embedded as it is with Chinese philosophy, traditions, and wisdom, we never reject any Western ideas such as competency models. In fact, we strongly encourage the inclusion of diverse ideas from all over the world.

Endnote

1. Muller, Charles A. *The Analects of Confucius*. June 6, 2013. Web, September 19, 2014 at www.acmuller.net/con-dao/analects.html.

Chapter 5

High Trust Environment

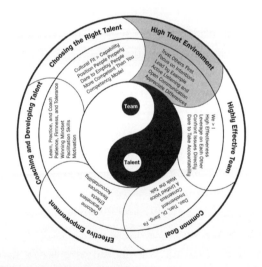

High Trust Environment

- Trust Others First
- Focus on Intentions
- Lead by Example
- Active Listening and Open Communication
- Appreciate Differences

If *Choosing the Right Talent* is the prerequisite for a company's sustainability, then a *High Trust Environment* is the fertile ground needed to nurture talent and effective teamwork.

High Trust Environment refers to the cohesion and cooperation among team members. It relies on mutual understanding, support, and willingness to care for others and appreciate each other's differences at the workplace.

A team without a trusting work setting will cultivate an uninspiring atmosphere, one that breeds cold relationships among team members and heightened sensitivity. Within such a working environment, employees will only feel oppressed and become less enthusiastic. In turn they will not be able to maximize their productivity and potential, thus lowering effectiveness.

Contrary to this scenario, a powerful level of trust creates mutual respect and understanding among team members. When team members trust each other, everyone can work easily in a relaxed environment, have open communication, and be willing to help one another. This working style will help strive toward a *Common Goal*. Creativity and productivity will both exponentially increase.

In the same way as you would like to be assessed by others, you should never judge or make quick assumptions about others' motives. Instead, you should always try to practice attentive listening, to take the initiative in trusting others, and to proactively create an atmosphere with higher levels of trust and support before expecting others to trust in you. What we advocate in our company is the idea of *Leading by Example*.

Only when the atmosphere generates high levels of trust can we maximize the utility of teamwork, and producing synergy, which yields $1 + 1 > 2$. Only with a *Common Goal* in mind are we able to become a united force to create miracles.

In our company, when a supervisor phones a subordinate it is very common to hear the supervisor first ask "Is it convenient to talk now?" or "I hope I'm not intruding," rather than bluntly asking "Where are you now?" or "What are you doing?" or directly assigning tasks. These considerate gestures reflect mutual respect, the value of thinking from others' perspectives, and the trust among our employees.

In a *High Trust Environment*, supervisors should not only be *Choosing the Right Talent* but also be giving subordinates the space they need to accomplish their duties on their own. In addition, supervisors should never question their subordinates too much but rather provide their subordinates with necessary support and coaching. Instead of directly interfering with their employees' duties, a leader should fully trust the people to complete their tasks efficiently and meet their deadlines.

Trust Others First

I want to share with you the importance of trust and the way it constitutes the foundation of a functioning society. What is the key to building trust? From my personal experience, it is to *Trust Others First*.

I remember my boarding high school days in the United States. I would always hide my cash allowance in the nooks and crannies of my dorm room. One day, I found that some of my allowance was missing. At the time, one dorm room hosted four students, and two of my roommates and I grew extremely suspicious of the last roommate of ours. So the three of us questioned him firmly, yet he insisted that he never stole the money. We even ended up beating him. I soon forgot about the whole incident. However, one day, when I was packing my things, I found the missing allowance stuffed in the pocket of one of my shirts. At that moment, I was shattered and realized it was a misunderstanding. I had made a huge mistake in beating up my poor roommate for no reason.

I never forgot about this event because it taught me a profound lesson that I carried throughout the rest of my life. I should never make any rash assumptions about anyone and should *Trust Others First* lest I end up doing something I would regret.

There was a questionnaire on trust that I once came across. Its results demonstrated that almost everyone hoped to get trust and respect from others, but that it was unlikely that a person would take the initiative to have faith in others first. In reality, many people are waiting to earn others' trust, yet they do not want to take the first step. Ultimately, we are left with a world infected with suspicion and distrust. Therefore, to build reliance on each other and create a *High Trust Environment*, we must first take the initiative to believe in others and credit that their intentions are good.

Trusting Others First has its risks, but distrusting others may bring about even greater harm. Just imagine a business where employees never trusted each other, creating a perpetual cycle of checking and being checked. This is a problem in itself. It will create a huge waste of resources and will severely reduce the efficiency of the company's operations. More importantly, a distrusting environment produces large amounts of psychological stress—no one enjoys the feeling of having to look over their shoulder at all times. This would sequentially affect employees' health, diminish their productivity, and increase the company's expenses. Therefore, the cost of mistrust in others is incredibly high.

If an employer first believes in their employees, assuming that the employees are always well intentioned for the company's benefit, this trust will make employees feel respected. Moreover, it will mutually inspire passion for and faith in the company while increasing productivity.

Focus on Intentions

Perhaps you will relate to the next story I am about to share with you.

One day, a father came home late from work and was feeling very exhausted. His five-year-old son was still awake and kept pestering his father for $10. At this time, his father became very angry and said, "I know you just want to buy toys, just go to bed now!"

After a while, his father regretted raising his voice at his son and opened his door to give him the $10 he had asked for. His son happily went under his pillow to present another $10 and gave both $10 bills to his father. He smiled and said to his father, "You once told me that you made $20 an hour. Now that I have $20, can I buy an hour of your time to have dinner with me?"

The father made a rash assumption that his son wanted the money to spend on toys. Yet in reality, the child only wanted his father to spend some quality time with him. The moral of this story is that we should never make quick assumptions about others' intentions because they could possibly lead to wrong conclusions and blaming others unjustly. The most important gift is to be able to always consider the motivation behind others' actions.

Focusing on Intentions refers to starting your thought process by considering the reasons behind others' actions. In real life, our specific positions, emotions, and other facets affect our way of making judgments. When analyzing a situation, we usually base our assumptions on actions and stereotypes. On the flip side, when we analyze our own actions, we emphasize our sources of motivation rather than our behaviors.

Each September, our company develops work plans and budgets for the coming year. Yet, often in the second year, some staff members will submit applications for additional budgets. By simply judging their behavior, we might have accused them of not planning well in advance and labeled them as big spenders, and reject their application. This may dampen their enthusiasm for work, resulting in the company missing out on other great opportunities. Therefore, we tend not to reject applications for additional budgets lightly. Instead, we pay more attention to the contents of the application to see if it runs along the company's objectives. Moreover, our company sets aside a reserve fund annually to meet justifiable extra budget applications. Ultimately, if the intentions of our employees were selfish and self-interested, bringing losses to the company, those budget applications would surely be rejected.

Also, only because of *Focusing on Intentions* can we truly solidify our foundation of trust. Our employees are more willing to share, assume greater responsibility, and be more innovative. Without *Focusing on Intentions*, there would be a lot of mismanagement as well as blame being tossed around.

Furthermore, this would harm the team's cohesion and damage everyone's dedication and passion.

Focusing on Intentions is not an easy task. Since we are more accustomed to judging others by their behavior instead of considering their true motives, we need to be more conscious of *Focusing on Intentions* and trying to understand the incentives behind others' actions.

Lead by Example

Lead by Example means being able to accomplish something yourself before asking others to do the same.

Being able to follow through with your words through concrete action is a basis for building trust. Behavior is powerful and pragmatic for convincing others that you can be a good leader. If you are a person that can *Lead by Example,* others can easily identify with your character and your working style. They can give you a sense of acknowledgment, support you, and become more willing to cooperate with you.

You can hardly imagine a world where managers smoke in the workplace but prohibit employees from smoking; or where supervisors are late to meetings, but require staff to be punctual. We have a saying in Chinese, "上行下效," that means subordinates usually imitate their superiors. It is much easier to learn from negative habits than positive ones. Therefore, we emphasize the importance of the higher levels of staff to *Lead by Example.*

For example, as we mentioned in building a *High Trust Environment*, if a supervisor is dishonest during a background-sharing session or chooses not to share honestly, this interaction makes it extremely difficult for their subordinates to trust in the supervisor and open up to them.

As another example, we often say that trusting in subordinates allows us to effectively utilize their strengths and unlock their potential. If a supervisor delegates a task to their subordinates but doubts their abilities or perhaps even jumps in to complete the task, they break the bond of trust between supervisor and employees. The supervisor's behavior will seriously jeopardize the teamwork in their working environment.

There is a Chinese proverb, "言傳不如身教," which accords with the English idiom of "Actions speak louder than words." In our company, I am dedicated to setting a good example. In trusting my management team, I hope that they can both effectively complete their assignments and trust their subordinates in accomplishing their respective tasks. Whenever we run into any disagreements or problems, I patiently listen to my staff and allow them adequate room to perform. Even when I have my own opinions, I tend to hold back, letting my employees do what they think is right for the company to strive in terms of our *High Trust Environment* and *Positioning People Properly*.

I believe in setting myself as a role model. This way, if I can accomplish something so can my top management team. If my top management team can do the same, then their subordinates can also achieve equally as well.

Active Listening and Open Communication

Breaking down the structure of the Chinese word for "listen," "聽," we can see how one's eyes (目), ears (耳), and heart (心) are used in listening. To create a *High Trust Environment*, *Active Listening* and *Open Communication* are crucial.

Listening can also be a mode of silent communication. *Active Listening* reflects our sincere attitude and respect for others, which should be kept in mind at all times. Through *Active Listening*, we can understand a person's character, background, thoughts, and decipher their motives. By using this information as a stepping-stone, we can start to pinpoint areas for improvement and figure out the best solution.

Besides the formal aspect, *Active Listening* is also the first step in unlocking someone's heart. It makes us experience friendship and compassion, pulling people closer together by increasing trust and support to create a *High Trust Environment*.

Our company conducts an employee satisfaction survey annually to understand our staff's opinions on the implementation of our corporate culture. In addition it includes their feedforward on our work processes, salary, benefits, and the progress of reaching a balance between health, family, and work. Afterwards, we persist in improving ourselves based on the findings of those surveys. For over ten years now, the surveys have become a vital part of our institution as we strive to actively listen to the many voices in our company.

We often use the phrases "What do you think?" and "What is your opinion?" to encourage everyone to put their heads together, to proactively voice their opinions, and to point out issues when necessary. Even when our colleagues bring up a seemingly simple problem, we discourage cutting them off midsentence and instead promote understanding of their point of view to bring different voices and opinions together.

Going above and beyond listening, we moreover provide productive feedforward and *Open Communication*. What we mean by *Open Communication* is the way we open our mind to directly and candidly express our thoughts while being considerate of each other's feelings.

Contrary to the groups of people who are very vague in expressing their opinions and like to avoid issues, we hope to foster a community that is more willing to accept and trust each other, and to honestly express their opinions. Therefore, *Active Listening and Open Communication* are key concepts in building a *High Trust Environment*.

Our company promotes a *Team Communication Model* that lists in detail the "dos" and "don'ts" when conducting *Open Communication*. We have turned the contents of our *Team Communication Model* into posters, like the one displayed on the previous page, everywhere around the office. Sometimes, facilitators of meetings will use this model as a guideline in facilitating a conference, pointing directly to the "do's" and "don'ts."

In my opinion, a harmonious and cohesive team is able to actively listen, accept different opinions, and voice opinions

Team Communication Model

Do	Don't
We > I	Responding with Negative Emotion
Express Honestly	Dominate the Discussion
Feedforward	Listen Subjectively
Speak Openly	Refuse to Change
Debate Proactively	Say One Thing and Do Another
Judge the Matter and not the Individual	Personally Attack Others

openly, providing for each member a sense of belonging and energy to take part in building this *High Trust Environment*.

Appreciate Differences

Every person has their unique personality, background, education, way of thinking, and work experience. Therefore, the world does not have a uniform model of how a person should be. These differences are a positive thing as they allow each one of us to bring out our unique strengths.

If one cannot accept, tolerate, or *Appreciate Differences*, but rather sees others' differences as drawbacks, it will be difficult to build trust. Appreciating differences and embracing diversity builds mutual recognition and trust rather than instigating conflict. Through this appreciation, we can find complementing talents from each other's unique identity to bolster interdependence, mutual encouragement, and effectively utilize resources to realize $1 + 1 > 2$. Of course, appreciating differences has its limits in our corporate context as we also place a heavy emphasis on cultural fit.

The renowned management expert Peter Drucker once said, "Whenever anything is being accomplished, it is being done, I have learned, by a monomaniac with a mission."[1] Drucker raises a very interesting point, that a business needs to have a variety of talented people who can think outside the box. Every employee can sharpen one's unique skills and synergize with others as an effective team.

Our employees come from all walks of life. The diversity within our working community is extremely vast, and if we do not take the time to mutually respect and appreciate each other's differences, we will have difficulty in communicating effectively and working together.

Only through mutual appreciation can we really learn to accommodate and work with each other respectfully. Otherwise, it is hard to imagine that people with contrasting personalities who do not identify with each other will openly communicate and have good faith when working with each other. Only heartfelt appreciation can bring everyone a sense of mutual trust, in which companies can retain talented people and unlock their true talents.

Endnote

1. Hurst, David K. "Monomaniacs with a Mission." *Strategy + Business.* November 16, 2001. Web, September 19, 2014 at www.strategy-business.com/article/11228?pg=all.

Chapter 6

Highly Effective Team

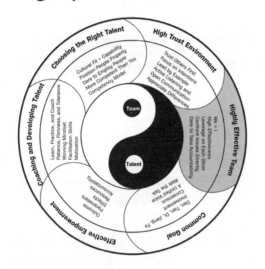

Highly Effective Team

- We > I
- High Effectiveness
- Leverage on Each Other
- Confront Issues Directly
- Dare to Take Accountability

Along with *Choosing the Right Talent* and creating a *High Trust Environment*, team members also need to be able to leverage off each other's strengths and focus on results. In striving for high effectiveness, they must form a *Highly Effective Team* in order to compete, turn challenges into opportunities, and maintain an advantage.

The *Highly Effective Team* we mention here refers to a team that emphasizes establishing a *Common Goal*, owning responsibility, and building mutual trust. In addition, the team focuses on results and pursues high effectiveness and productivity. Specifically, a successful group should possess mutual appreciation and support among team members, which will maximize everyone's unique talents. When faced with a problem, team members should collectively find a solution and *Dare to Take Accountability*. When taking any action, team members should always consider the perspective of the group and efficiently pursue a *Common Goal*.

In a team, how each member understands their responsibilities, the team's organization, and structure can vary. Therefore, only when everyone understands the unique characteristics of the group and persistently advances those specific skills can a team create synergy and become a *Highly Effective Team*. Once the team members feel a sense of belonging, they will rarely oppose collaboration and will instead fully commit to the cause and encourage each other.

Nevertheless, while we recognize both the necessity and the risks of trusting others, how then can we build a *Highly Effective Team*? How do we encourage individuals to recognize their strengths yet also appreciate the power of teamwork? How do we motivate everyone to acquire the drive to help others? How do we collect everyone's strengths to yield twice the results with half the effort and achieve $1 + 1 > 2$? How should a team deal with conflict? These are some of the questions this chapter will try to answer.

We > I

The conference began but an employee came late because he had not finished his assignments. While the other dozens of employees sat around the conference room waiting for him, in effect, he wasted dozens of people's precious minutes.

Some employees clearly witnessed the oversights of their fellow colleagues but felt no accountability and therefore chose to ignore them.

The two scenarios given above show the "I" perspective. This point of view does not consider the "We" viewpoint, completely neglecting the entire ideal of *We > I*. When personal interests outweigh group benefits, this selfishness may bring harm to the entire group, in which everyone would suffer its negative consequences. *We > I* means considering the company's overall wellbeing as something greater than any individual's interests. It means emphasizing the importance of us striving for a greater collective good. Therefore, *We > I* is imperative in ensuring the effective functioning of a team.

The concept of *We* > *I* also embodies the message that "We" can bring much greater value to the table than "I" can on my own. Collaborative wisdom and strength are far superior to those of a single person, which alludes to our notion of $1 + 1 > 2$.

We > *I* helps foster a heightened mindset for solving problems and taking control of situations. Often, if we simply look from our own perspective to solve problems, it is almost impossible to find the perfect answer. Only when you stand at a higher level with a more complete perspective can you see new possibilities and find superior solutions. If everyone only looked through their own perspective, then it would be impossible to form a *Highly Effective Team.*

Football fans will know the serious consequences of a player who focuses solely on his own performance and scoring. His unwillingness to cooperate with his team members or rejection of his coach's strategies could negatively impact the entire team's performance. The team may even lose the game.

In another case, a company is about to launch a new product and the sales department hopes to bring it to market in three months. However, the production department's thorough assessments maintain that the preparation of raw materials will require at least six months to reach the final target. If the two departments merely stand in their own shoes, reject each other's perspectives, and refuse to compromise, the failed attempt to launch this new product will jeopardize the entire company.

In these situations, we usually convene a special interdepartmental meeting to look at the situation. We carefully analyze, repeatedly discuss, and identify the key points to solve the problem. Following that, we come up with estimates for developing programs to finally reach a *Consensus* on launching new products into the market.

This new time horizon could deviate from the initial three-month or six-month benchmark and could be four months instead. In my opinion, there is no right or wrong answer as to when is the best time to launch a new product. The key is that everyone should reach an agreement for the benefit of the entire company. The agreement must be able to fulfill the market's expectations and demands and not affect the original production plans. I believe this method produces the best results.

There is no perfect person, but there are perfect teams. Strong cooperation unlocks the full potential of the team's strengths, demonstrating the power of *We > I.*

High Effectiveness

There are many companies that promote high efficiency, but in our company we advocate *High Effectiveness.*

While efficiency emphasizes speed, effectiveness accentuates results. On one hand, efficiency concentrates on the time it takes to solve a problem or finish a task. On the other hand, effectiveness pursues completing projects with the least amount of time, financial, and human capital in order to reap the best possible results.

Many mistake a busy employee for a highly efficient employee because of the extra hours put into their work. However, being busy or working overtime does not necessarily mean *High Effectiveness.* To exemplify, given the same assignment, an employee that uses less time than another can produce even more effective results. A person with higher work effectiveness is able to enjoy the *Three Balances of Life—Health, Family, Work* while completing the project on time.

However, effectiveness is all about results and not about speed or efficiency. "Slow is fast, fast is slow." This is the motto we use to remind our staff that we would rather see great results with less speed than mediocre results with high speed. No one should jeopardize outcome for immediacy.

For example, when a company assigns project-based work to its employees, the general practice is to determine the right personnel, objectives, and deadline, and then let everyone start work immediately.

On the contrary, our company frequently assigns many cross-departmental projects. Before we establish the project teams, we spend a lot of time selecting the right personnel by clearly communicating with these employees and their supervisors. The purpose is to clarify their responsibilities and gain their full support before proceeding. After the project groups are established, we do not rush everyone into working. Instead, we conduct team-building activities, such as self-introductions and background sharing, to increase team members' mutual trust and understanding, and to create a *High Trust Environment*. Then, we proceed to set a *Common Goal*, to define the division of labor, formulate a concrete plan of action, and finally commence operations.

Perhaps some may think that it is a waste of time to take so long to select the right teams, to communicate clearly, and to conduct team-building activities, yet we believe the opposite.

From our perspective, by taking the time to pick the right people, to set up mutual understanding and trust, communication will be smooth. Subsequently, conflict will be reduced, work effectiveness will increase, and this will guarantee and support progress. On the surface, the start of the process may seem slow, but once these foundations are laid, the overall process will not only speed up but also make the results more effective.

Our company's objective of *High Effectiveness* is also reflected in our development strategy. All along, we have focused on striking a balance between long-term and short-term interest as well as between the company's benefits and social responsibility. We do not attempt to expand to the far limit, nor do we set overambitious goals and deadlines. In this way, we can ensure that the results will be an accumulation of steady and productive growth, creating a sustainable foundation for the company to keep advancing.

Leverage on Each Other

You may have heard the following interesting story.

A blind man and a physically disabled man lived together. One day, their house caught fire. The blind man had to feel around to find an exit, but failed. The physically disabled man could see the exit but he could not escape right away and had to take the smallest steps to inch towards it. As the fire intensified, if they did not run away immediately, the flames would consume them. At this critical moment, the blind man carried the disabled man while the disabled man gave the blind man directions toward the exit. Thus, the two quickly escaped the sea of flames and were well out of danger.

The moral of the story is that everyone has their own strengths and weaknesses. While you need to leverage off each other's strengths, it is also crucial to help others as well.

In fact, life is all about *Leveraging on Each Other*. As we receive daily guidance and services from others, we should also do the same for others.

In every company, each department specializes in its own field and has varying responsibilities, resources, and strengths. Only through *Leveraging on Each Other*, combining resources, and forming a complete workflow can teams support each other to maintain the smooth operation of a company. In a team, even if there is one individual who is extremely competent, that person still has weaknesses. Even if they have incredible energy, they still cannot complete everything alone. Only through the power of teamwork can an ultimate goal be reached.

Leveraging on Each Other has two facets--you help others and others help you.

In a team, when others run into obstacles like having a shortage of people or resources, we must proactively share our own resources, and intelligence, and lend a hand to help others achieve their goals in a spirit of *We > I*. When others are depressed, discouraged, fatigued mentally and physically, we must take the initiative to help and to encourage them to keep going.

Care, encouragement, and recognition may be just the spiritual strength that is most needed by others, which is another way of *Leveraging on Each Other*.

Helping others is not difficult, yet proactively asking others for help can be challenging. Many people hold "Never ask for help" as one of their work principles. They believe that asking for help is bothersome to others, that owing others favors is tedious, and that others may criticize their competence.

In my opinion, leveraging off others is not necessarily troublesome. Rather, it lets others know that you have trust in them. If they succeed in helping you, they will in turn feel accomplished. Leveraging off others is not at all shameful. Everyone runs into obstacles and problems they cannot solve themselves. *Leveraging on Each Other* is an act of standing in the perspective of the team, in the view of *We > I*, breaking through the constraints of the "I" perspective. It takes skill, courage, and intellect. Hence, we always say, to *Leverage on Each Other* makes work and life much easier.

Confront Issues Directly

We all know that a straight line is the shortest distance between two points. Similarly, from the roots of a problem to its resolution, *Confronting Issues Directly* is the most effective way of solving problems.

However, Chinese people are typically very concerned with "saving face," so they never mention anything when they find a problem with others' work. They prefer only to speak about it privately or hesitate to voice their own opinions. The result is collapsed communication: the opposing side fails to recognize the problem, or just partially acknowledges it. When encountering problems, some may be reluctant to ask someone else for help. Many would instead bury their head in the sand like ostriches, taking the most evasive attitude and resolution, or not solving any problems at all.

This way of avoiding problems or using an indirect way of resolving a problem will worsen the situation, increase the difficulty and cost of solving it, or even let the most opportune time slip away, leading to serious consequences.

When looking at the same problem, people may have diverse approaches and views, which is completely normal. The best way to avoid disagreements and conflict is to *Confront Issues Directly* through direct communication rather than hiding our feelings or requiring middlemen. This will all help avoid distortion of information so that we can quickly understand what is going on and quickly find a solution.

✗ **Don't**   ✓ **Do**

Confronting Issues Directly is the only way to avoid mistrust and misunderstandings, to build trust, to simplify complicated situations, and to solve problems with *High Effectiveness.*

In tackling a problem, we must especially emphasize not casting doubt on others' motives, and instead believing in their good intentions. At the same time, we should not worry about others' skepticism about our own intentions.

Therefore, our company encourages people to speak the truth and to have open communication. On the other hand, we discourage using middlemen, making rash assumptions about other's motives, and launching personal attacks.

Of course, when we point out the problem to others and resolve it, we must be empathetic and try to understand other's feelings. Mutual respect and mutual understanding should be built so as to maintain the team's high level of trust.

Dare to Take Accountability

In my opinion, the courage to *Dare to Take Accountability* has two levels of meaning.

The first level is to have the initiative to take on additional work to share the entire team's pressures and responsibilities. The second level is to have the courage to admit mistakes, dare to take responsibility, confront issues head on, and create preventive measures to avoid recurrence.

When a person constantly challenges themselves by taking on additional obligations, they capture more opportunities to display their talents, to persistently grow, to make greater contributions, and to broaden their horizons.

Everyone takes on different roles and assumes varying tasks when working in a team. If we can think in terms of the entire team's interest and not just individual interest and try our best to perform our duties, this will be the best way to *Dare to Take Accountability* as a responsible member of the team.

If a team can collectively stand in the perspective of "We," take the initiative to share more work and to accept more challenging tasks, then the members of the team can work cohesively and unlock their collective gifts. The sense of accomplishment and sense of belonging from completing tasks as a team lets everyone feel the value of their contribution. This realization enhances trust, teamwork, and effectiveness.

The following phenomenon exists in our company as well.

When confronted with a problem, we usually hold interdepartmental meetings to analyze the roots of the problem together and find a solution to it. Some people may subconsciously explain their specific roles and responsibilities, emphasize their compliance with directions and requirements, and prove their irrelevance to the problem's cause.

If this happens, the meeting will digress as everyone continues to look for reasons while trying to shift blame away. Therefore, the meeting that was originally supposed to solve the issue will turn into a meeting with many complaints and mutual accusations. Eventually, everyone will forget about the problem-solving reason of the meeting in the first place.

In fact, problems themselves are nothing to be afraid of. The real fear is the lack of direct confrontation, the lack of responsibility, or the attempts to cover up the problem. If, at this time, someone proactively said, "Sorry, I did not do a good job," or "It was my responsibility, sorry for the inconvenience," then the scenario would have ended differently. Everyone would show their understanding of the situation. Everyone would empathize, care, and reassure the responsible individual. Team members would not shift blame back and forth. In fact, they would work together to find a solution to the problem.

In my opinion, when the problem has already materialized, there is no way to alter the facts. We can only accept and face it. This is a crucial time to find a positive solution rather than sorting out accountability. If we can prevent similar issues from happening again with the lessons learned, then this predicament may actually be a blessing.

Needless to say, this does not mean that an employee does not need to bear the consequences of their mistakes. We first consider their intentions. Let us say that the employee was motivated by the group's interest and not their personal interest, but lack of experience and of an all-rounded perspective led to the errors. In this case, we treat the mistakes as the employee's areas for improvement and hope that they will not repeat their oversight. On the other hand, if personal interest motivated this employee, or if they refused to be accountable for their faults, or even if they offended the code of others, then we would hold the employee liable for their errors.

Chapter 7

Common Goal

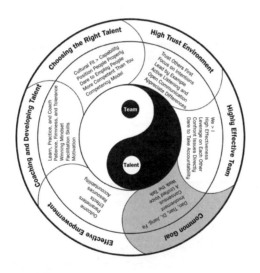

Common Goal

- *Dao, Tian, Di, Jiang, Fa (道, 天, 地, 將, 法)*
- Involvement
- Consensus
- A Unified Voice
- Walk the Talk

I enjoy watching football matches not just for the excitement, but also because it brings about introspection. Football is not only amusing to spectators anticipating its unpredictable outcome, but the sport's strategic aspect in coordinating teamwork also stimulates the viewer's analytical reasoning.

During the 2002 FIFA World Cup hosted by Korea and Japan, the Korean team's performance was unforgettable. Despite the fact that they did not have superstar players in their lineup, even against the toughest opponents the entire team played very aggressively and collaborated very well. Ultimately, the seemingly weak Korean team shocked the audience by qualifying for the semi-finals. It was a miracle. I personally believe that the reason why the Korean team succeeded was that they had a *Common Goal*—"Victory."

What is a *Common Goal*?

A *Common Goal* refers to an objective set collaboratively by a group of people. It directs everyone in what to do and embeds the reasoning behind it. A team can ensure the achievement of its shared objective by cooperating with *unified hearts and actions*.

A collective target is the direction of a team's efforts, the motivation of a team's perseverance, and the glue that binds its members together. It can inspire team members to unlock their extensive potential to charge creativity, vitality, passion, and a sense of mission and responsibility.

If there were no *Common Goal*, a team would be like a ship lost at sea without a destination in mind. Members would have no idea what to do or how to cooperate with each other. Moreover, they could lose their sense of value and lose the will to persevere.

Some entrepreneurs and leaders like setting goals behind closed doors and merely let their employees implement those objectives. However, our company believes that setting a *Common Goal* requires general participation and *Consensus*. Collaborative goal setting brings about passion and cohesion. This method gives employees a sense of belonging and respect. It provides the platform to showcase their talents and to unlock their unlimited potential. In addition, participation advocates uniformity and teamwork, and ensures accurate execution with a clear direction in mind. Furthermore, the success in achieving goals together charges everyone with an incredible sense of accomplishment.

Dao, Tian, Di, Jiang, Fa (道, 天, 地, 將, 法)

What is *Dao, Tian, Di, Jiang, Fa (道, 天, 地, 將, 法)*?

> It comes from *The Art of War:* "兵者, 國之大事, 死生之地, 存亡之道, 不可不察也。故經之以五事, 校之以計, 而索其情: 一曰道, 二曰天, 三曰地, 四曰將, 五曰法"[1]

Dao, Tian, Di Jiang, Fa (道, 天, 地, 將, 法) are the five vital aspects a military commander must consider in order to attain victory in the context of war. These five aspects are the way, weather, terrain, commander, and discipline. We came up with our own application of these simple key points for corporate use to generate our own strategic development model.

In our strategic thinking platform, *Dao (道)* refers to a *Common Goal* and direction. *Tian (天)* means the external variables. *Di (地)* refers to the internal variables. *Jiang (將)* means *Choosing the Right Talent,* and *Fa (法)* refers to method.

When putting this model into action we take the following steps.

First, we analyze the *Current Profile* of our company. Next, we look at the *Tian (天)* and *Di (地)*, the external variables and the internal variables. Following, we depict our *Future Profile* together with our *Common Goal* and direction, which is the *Dao (道)* aspect or the definition of success. Next, we evaluate the difference between our *Current Profile* and our *Future Profile*. Then, we choose a method, the *Fa (法)*, to achieve the *Future Profile*. Finally, we assign project owners, allowing them to find their own productive approach, which symbolizes the *Jiang (將)* part.

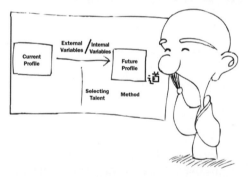

Next, I will use the example of launching a new product to explain how we use this platform for strategic thinking.

First, we analyze the *Current Profile* of the product: the products that are successful and those that are not, as well as the reasons behind. Next, we analyze the *Tian*—the external conditions and upcoming trends, such as demographic changes, the trend of consumer demand, and application of new technology. In addition, we conduct studies on existing competitors, including their strengths, weaknesses, and strategic positioning. Based on the above information, we draw implications on how to develop our products. We then evaluate the *Di*—the strengths and weaknesses of our company's products. Following, we determine the *Dao* of our new product development, which is the definition of success. These can be measured by indexes such as sales amount, repeated purchases, customer satisfaction rate, and so on. We proceed to figure out what the *Future Profile* should look like. Such features as development direction, product mix, and pricing of the new product are considered. Last, we select the right leader, *Jiang*, to invent the method, *Fa*, to bridge the gap between the "current" and the "future."

Prior to using *Dao (道)*, *Tian (天)*, *Di (地)*, *Jiang (將)*, *Fa (法)* as our platform for strategic thinking, our company's meetings were often very heated: When it came to where to start in developing a strategy, what problems to consider, what approaches to use, what the desired end result would be, everyone had differing opinions and views. Sometimes meetings would last for days at a time, as there were too many ideas being brought up, which made it challenging to create results. However, once we came up with this new platform, we had a common channel, a unified language, and a common wavelength to reach a consensus.

This strategic thinking platform can also help the leader concentrate more on *Dao (道)*, *Tian (天)*, *Di (地)*, *Jiang (將)*, while less on *Fa (法)* alone.

Currently, this platform has been widely adopted for all aspects of strategic thinking in our company, from departmental strategies to project planning.

We also used this tool to develop our company's third five-year development plan. In each five-year plan, we clearly and carefully set the company's future development strategic plan and depict the future profile. We resolve problems that we foresee in the next half-decade about what we should and should not work on with respect to corporate culture, talent, products, branding, and other important aspects.

Our company's five-year strategic plan is our *Common Goal*. With this collaborative objective, our company can push forward in the same direction; employees have a common vision, mission, and a sense of ownership. With this shared purpose, even when faced with obstacles, employees will not shatter, back down, or give up. With this shared objective in mind, employees will be full of passion, confidence, and endless creativity to work together to lead the company to healthy and promising growth.

Involvement

Setting goals is not difficult, but turning these goals into reality is no easy task.

In my opinion, the key in turning objectives into reality is to let every team member try their best to achieve the company's *Common Goal* parallel to their personal goals. They must recognize and support this collective purpose whole-heartedly.

The best way is to get everyone involved in setting a group goal. In the team, every member wants to demonstrate their value to the company. If they can participate in the decision-making process, have their opinions acknowledged and feel personally connected to the issue, then they will be more enthusiastic in contributing their ideas, resources, understanding, and support.

Therefore, when setting goals, we usually gather the individual objectives of the relevant employees and encourage them to fully voice their opinions.

For example, we establish our annual sales target as follows.

Every July, our company launches an annual strategic review through questionnaires, conferences, and focus group meetings to listen to different departments, front-line staff, and customers. At the same time, the sales department produces related forecasts based on business intelligence. In September, the business department integrates the views of all parties, analyzes data, and provides an estimate of next year's sales target. This is submitted to the core management team for discussion and feedback. Based on this feedback, a new round of communication and revision is conducted, until the core management team approves the final report.

Through the *Involvement* of our staff in deliberations as well as bottom-up and top-down communication, we finally succeed in setting an annual sales target. This goal is no longer decided solely by the leader, but is instead worked out through everyone's combined efforts.

Perhaps some leaders will feel skeptical: Does allowing employees to take part in setting goals lead to lower standards and a static status quo?

From our corporate experience, this is not the case. Conversely, sometimes the *Common Goal* is even more challenging than what each individual has had in mind.

I believe in a company that highly respects its staff. It gives its employees a strong sense of belonging and promotes personal and corporate progress side by side. In that environment, employees will naturally consider their personal interests as well as the company's benefits. If an easy target is set, then the excitement from challenges is lost; employees will no longer have passion and fighting spirit. This is not a situation anyone would want. Furthermore, with the staff's involvement, everyone can contribute and work together, integrate individual experiences, different opinions, and intellect to improve and rationalize the company's objectives.

Consensus

There is a story called "The Princess' Moon."

A little princess fell ill and told the king that if she could have the moon, she would feel well again. The king immediately called on all the wise men around the nation and asked them to find a way to capture the moon.

One minister said, "The moon is thousands of miles away and its scale is much larger than the princess' room." The magician said, "The moon is 150,000 miles away, its size should be more than twice the palace." The mathematician said, "The moon is 30,000 miles away and is half the size of the entire kingdom. Also, it is stuck in the sky and we cannot grab the moon."

The king was extremely anxious and asked the clown to entertain the little princess. After understanding the situation, the clown realized that everyone had a different perspective on the moon's shape, size, and distance. The key issue was to find what the moon meant to the little princess herself.

The clown immediately asked the little princess, to which she replied, "The moon is smaller than a thumbnail, it is golden, and hangs on the trees." So the king commanded the production of a little "moon" made in gold for the little princess as a necklace pendant. The princess was very happy and her illness went away the next day.

The Princess' Moon

In fact, situations similar to the story of "The Princess' Moon" happen frequently at the workplace. Everyone debates because contentions and conflicts may arise thanks to the different "moons" we believe in, where one person's "moon" is completely unlike another's.

Reaching a 100 percent *Consensus* is the ideal of decision making. But it is a rare occurrence. With everyone's specific opinions and interpretations of our goals, it is difficult to reach a unanimous decision all the time. Instead, we encourage active discussions to reach a mutual understanding and a final decision.

If there were no agreement between managers and their subordinates, it would be nearly impossible to unify the team. It might even lead to widespread individualism, negating the group's goals, creating disorder and inefficiency, and ultimately failing to accomplish the objective.

It is important to keep in mind, however, that during discussions there should be respect for intellect, facts, and free expression of opinions. The team should avoid any biases and inequalities in order to figure out what is best for the collective. Reaching a united outlook, direction, and action plan is a participatory process, a collaborative journey, a process that emphasizes *We > I*, which creates a win-win situation.

A Unified Voice

Whenever a *Unified Voice* is brought up, I always like to share the following example.

When encountering a problem, we usually hold meetings to gather opinions and find a solution. However, not every meeting results in a united direction or plan of action. If there are seven out of ten people that vote for "left" and the remaining three vote for "right," with the time crunch the manager must make the final decision. Although a unanimous *Consensus* may not be reached, the manager should make a final call with the group's interest in mind and the support of all team members regardless of whether they voted for "right" or "left." Irrespective of the many obstacles the team may run into before finding a new and better resolution, they must always uphold and confirm the current decision altogether. This is what we refer to as owning a *Unified Voice*.

The main problem to avoid is holding back your opinions during the discussion period and then to complain about the results after the meeting has concluded. Another issue arises when someone says they agree with the final decision but when they run into obstacles during implementation, they go back on their word and complain about the decision made.

This inconsistent and contradictory behavior should be banned in the process of working as a team. It weakens our group decision, lowers confidence, morale, trust, and cooperation. It may even lead to failure in reaching the target.

We therefore advocate setting aside each other's differences when reaching a collective decision. We should stand in the perspective of the team. Instead of wasting time defining what is right and wrong, we should concentrate on action and results to create a *Highly Effective Team* to strive for a *Common Goal.*

Walk the Talk

In Chapter 6 on the *Highly Effective Team*, I have shared the example of launching a new product. In this example, the four-month time frame to launch is the group decision reached by the sales and production department in alignment with the *Common Goal.*

Let us assume that everyone recognizes and supports the *Consensus.* However, imagine that in implementation, the production department goes back on its word. They fall back on their original plan to purchase and produce but neglect to adjust the interdepartmental plan with the sales department. In addition, the sales department also ignores the agreement and comes up with a brand new product launch campaign, training, and other related work. In this way, the two departments' actions are contradictory to the collective agreement and hence do not meet the requirement of *Walk the Talk.*

To *Walk the Talk* is to follow through with a common objective by actively supporting the project, following the pre-set guidelines in implementation, and staying consistent with the initial agreement in order to ensure success in pursuing the shared purpose.

Some employees may not say no to the group decision and deeply support it. They, however, later find excuses to quibble or do not do their best. This would exemplify the opposite of *Walk the Talk*. Some employees may have different opinions on the communal decision but for unaccounted reasons they may verbally agree with the decision while acting in a contradictory manner. This conflicting behavior jeopardizes the shared objective, which is equivalent to not reaching a resolution at all, failing to practice what you preach.

The greatest harm of violating *Walk the Talk* is the disabling of a *High Trust Environment*, stirring up distrust. This breaks down cooperation, deviates from the common direction, and fails to pursue the *Common Goal*. More importantly, it sends the wrong signal to everyone: Implementation is not always consistent with decisions and commitments made, which reinforces distrust.

On the contrary, if employees *Walk the Talk*, and take concrete steps to support the group decision to reach the *Common Goal*, then it is possible to enhance mutual trust and cooperation between teams and improve the effectiveness of the company.

Endnote

1. 孫武.《孫子兵法》. 上海古籍出版社, 2009. Sun, Wu. *The Art of War*. Shanghai Chinese Classics Publishing House, 2009.

Chapter 8

Effective Empowerment

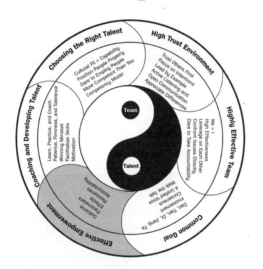

Effective Empowerment

- Outcome
- Parameters
- Effects
- Resources
- Accountability

In order to implement the team's *Common Goal*, you must first achieve *Effective Empowerment*. When delegating responsibilities to employees, you should also provide them with appropriate resources and support. This inspires everyone to realize one's talents as the synergy from teamwork can help achieve ultimate goals successfully.

Traditional management theory believes that empowerment is risky. Therefore, a lot of entrepreneurs and leaders are worried about and do not trust in delegating their work. However, the risk of not empowering and missing opportunities is higher than that of empowering.

Many companies are talking about empowerment, whereas our company advocates *Effective Empowerment*. Many managers practice empowerment by simply assigning jobs to their subordinates. On the contrary, managers who practice *Effective Empowerment* also coach their subordinates through systematic processes with the necessary guidelines, leading to more impressive results.

While a leader who refuses to or does not know how to effectively empower must micromanage constantly, a leader who grasps the way to leverage off their team will succeed without having to do all the hands-on work. The leader can expand the business with the help of their employees, which allows the leader to concentrate on strategic direction and creates a strong platform for employees to unleash their full potential and to achieve unexpected results.

So, are there any easy programs or guidelines to help us practice *Effective Empowerment*?

In conjunction with the other elements of the *Autopilot Leadership Model*, we have been using the tool OPERA and have achieved progressive results. This empowerment tool, explained by Larry Reynolds in his book *The Trust Effect: Creating the High Trust High Performance Organization*,[1] is simple, clear, and breaks down *Effective Empowerment* into five steps. OPERA is an acronym made up of the first letter of five English words that form the five steps to *Effective Empowerment*. Below, I will share the details of this tool with you and hope you can benefit from it as we have.

Outcome

The first step of *Effective Empowerment* is Outcome. It is very important to let employees clearly understand the desired outcome of the assignment so they can follow that direction during implementation. Communication breakdown stems from "people interpreting the same words in different ways." Therefore, it is imperative to have *Open Communication* between supervisors and subordinates to reach a *Consensus* before any plan of action. As exemplified in "The Princess' Moon," everyone's "moon" may not always be the same.

You may ask, "Isn't explaining the Outcome redundant if we have already set up a *Common Goal*?"

A *Common Goal* is more of a macro-objective. Further decomposition is needed in order to delegate accordingly to achieve this collective purpose. While everyone assumes different roles, it is vital to clarify the Outcome specifically to each individual based on their assignment.

Below, I will share an example of empowerment when a staff member is given the responsibility for organizing a New Year's party and will continue to introduce the application of OPERA in *Effective Empowerment*.

If a supervisor gives abstract directions to their subordinate about coordinating a New Year's party, the subordinate would have no clear objective to work towards. They would wonder: "What would be the measure of success for this New Year's party? What are the company's expectations of this party?"

To clearly state the desired Outcome, supervisors should prescribe the requirements, such as:

- Employee's Satisfaction Index > 85 points.
- Employee's Happiness Index > 90 points.
- Full participation of employees.

Only through measurable targets can the employee plan the specific tasks needed to complete the job. With a clear Outcome in mind, even when faced with unexpected situations, the employee can adjust accordingly to complete the project satisfactorily in a timely manner.

Parameters

The second step of OPERA is Parameters. This refers to designating clear boundaries and benchmarks to guide employees when they work on projects.

The supervisor should further include these parameters when assigning this New Year's party to the employee:

- It should be held before January 10th.
- All performances should be conducted by the staff—no outsourcing.
- The party venue should be no more than 30 minutes away by car from the company.

Defining Parameters helps specify the roles and responsibilities when effectively empowering someone so that they can concentrate on the task at hand without straying too far away.

Effects

The third step of OPERA is Effects—the importance, benefits of success, and the consequences of failure. This means explaining the purpose and impact of their work, the communal and personal benefits they would bring to the table, and the extent of personal development that could be achieved. At the same time, it also entails letting employees know how much they need to commit to their work and what sort of risks they may face.

Understanding the Effects motivates employees to face greater challenges with the comprehension of the importance and value of their work.

After outlining the Parameters of the New Year's party, the supervisor should inform their employee of the Effects of this assignment, such as:

- Help employees better understand the corporate culture.
- Show employees' talents, and enhance mutual understanding and trust.
- Build confidence and morale to accomplish the New Year's sales performance goals.

These benefits would be best explained and measured with specific scoring methods and indicators so that the employee knows the significance of their contributions.

Resources

The fourth step of OPERA is Resources. In addition to Outcome, Parameters, and Effects, employees require physical, financial, human, and time resources to complete their tasks. If you neglect to provide employees with the right resources, you will be setting them up for failure.

Tangible resources are not easily ignored. However, intangible resources like training and coaching can be very easily overlooked. Coaching not only gives employees timely advice, but also demonstrates supervisors' care, attention, and appreciation for their subordinates' hard work.

In helping the employee understand the Effects of the New Year's party, the supervisor should next give them the right resources, such as:

- $1 million budget.
- Staff from three different departments for help and support.
- 30 percent reduction in existing workload.
- Interviews with the employee once a week.

Employees will be well prepared to coordinate the New Year's party by using these resources effectively.

Accountability

After talking about Outcome, Parameters, Effect, and Resources, we come to the last element of OPERA—Accountability.

Employees should be required to make commitments to the key details of their projects like meeting the deadline, finding the accurate amount of resources needed, allocating resources, the expected results, and the way to measure how successful their project is.

After the communication between managers and staff, the employee should take accountability for their work in organizing the New Year's party:

- Complete the preparatory work within a month.
- Prevent the cost from exceeding the estimated budget of $1 million.
- Pay attention to the party attendees' level of satisfaction as reflection of their performance.

This exemplifies the staff member's commitment to the task, which indicates the ownership of accountability.

Of course, the supervisor and the employee can agree on when, where, and how to communicate with each other to determine the progress of the preparatory work. Yet, Accountability is all about the results and not the method. Employees should be free to use their creativity to make bold, innovative displays of their talents and strengths.

OPERA is a very simple five-step program. But without the implementation of all five steps, *Effective Empowerment* can prove to be a big challenge. Deprived of a clearly desired Outcome, employees have no direction. Without Parameters, there are no boundaries for employees to follow when completing their work. Lacking Effects, employees will not understand the effectiveness of their work. Without Resources, there would be empty and futile empowerment. In the absence of Accountability, employees will not show dedication and commitment to their work.

We emphasize the importance of aligning OPERA with our corporate culture. For example, when we explain the Outcome, supervisors usually listen to the opinions of their staff and reach a *Consensus* with them through *Open Communication*. When determining the deadline for employees to complete their tasks, we often consider their balance between health, family, and work instead of blindly setting deadlines. Hence, it is important that you use OPERA as a tool within your corporate culture structure.

Endnote

1. Reynolds, Lencioni. *The Trust Effect: Creating a High Trust High Performance Organization.* Nicholas Brealey Publishing, 1997.

Chapter 9

Coaching and Developing Talent

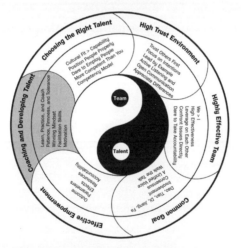

Coaching and Developing Talent

- Learn, Practice, and Coach
- Patience, Firmness, and Tolerance
- Winning Mindset
- Facilitation Skills
- Motivation

An excellent company not only needs talent, but also needs to build a talent pipeline. Only in this way can a team maintain dynamism, creativity, and the momentum to persistently reach new heights.

Learning and development studies from the past support the 70-20-10 Model.[1] It maintains that 70 percent of the successful development of talent comes from on-the-job training, while 20 percent comes from coaching, and the remaining 10 percent comes from classroom learning. Education on the job, leadership coaching, self-learning and correction, and repeated practice are all effective methods of nurturing talent.

Coaching and Developing Talent is not only a business strategy, but also a fundamental expectation of what leaders should and must do.

Coaching and Developing Talent creates a ripple effect, providing employees with development opportunities to unlock their potential, which ultimately helps them as well as the company grow. Managers provide the appropriate coaching much like a simple apprenticeship; the master passes on their experiences, skills, and knowledge to the apprentice by training the apprentice to mirror the master's practice and skills.

For example, when assigning projects, we typically pair up an employee with limited experience alongside a coach with extensive expertise. These coaches will observe, follow up, and support their employees' performance and effectiveness. Coaches do not provide concrete solutions to problems. Instead they support and inspire employees to discover their own answers. Through objective feedforward and advising, they encourage the team to explore their possibilities and recognize their own limitations.

This road to productive development generates respect among the team. More importantly, the talented people we train with this method do not become generic, mechanical, and rigid followers, but are independent thinkers who are unique and able to utilize their versatile talents in many ways.

Today, *Coaching and Developing Talent* has not only helped us nurture talented individuals, but has also created an environment in which everyone has the opportunity to become a coach. In this atmosphere, coaches continue to improve their abilities while those who are coached feel that the company values them and are inspired to exemplify coaching to others. Thus, everyone is willing to share their own experiences and to take on the roles of a coach or being coached.

Learn, Practice, and Coach

Although *Choosing the Right Talent* is a significant first step of the *Autopilot Leadership Model, Coaching and Developing Talent* is required to sustain the flow of talent. *Learn, Practice, and Coach* is one of the best methods to accomplish this.

Learn comprises of learning from others, from practice, and from teaching. *Practice* includes learning others' practices, the act of practicing itself, and teaching others. *Coach* encompasses teaching others to learn, to practice, and to teach.

Learn, Practice, and Coach is a cyclical process. Everyone is a learner as well as a teacher—this group of learners and teachers as a whole forms a bank that continuously accumulates knowledge, skills, and experience to boost development and inheritance. In learning something new, practicing it, and finally coaching others, these three steps tie the synergized loop of talent together and also build a strong sense of responsibility and commitment among employees without the need for special training programs.

When implementing *Learn, Practice, and Coach*, the coach plays a very important role. Our company has established interesting titles and customs: *Coaching the Head Coach*, *Peer Coaching*, and *Upward Coaching*.

We promote multiple levels of coaches no matter which post you are assigned to. You can have a *Coach*, a *Head Coach*, and even the *Coach of the Head Coach*. Our company believes that everyone at any level needs mentorship.

Ignoring the higher-ranked employees could jeopardize the system of cyclical learning. For example, the top management uses the Core Management Team meetings to give each other feedforward on areas for improvement. People form their own personal development plans for the coming year after integrating their peers' advice. This *Peer Coaching* approach through our feedforward method has worked effectively for over a decade.

Even as the CEO, I like to receive feedforward on my own performance from my Core Management Team to make necessary improvements. Selected employees are always the group who are most familiar with their supervisor's work performance, strengths, and weaknesses. And our employees' comments act as an effective mirror for their supervisors, which exemplify the role of a *Reverse Coach*.

I remember one time during a management meeting, there was a total of over 50 colleagues who participated and were divided into six groups. I especially arranged a session for everyone to discuss and evaluate my performance as the CEO, Managing Director, and Chairman with regard to direction, work ethic, time management, and leadership skills. They proceeded to give me feedforward by sending a representative per group to present their evaluation results. As each group spoke, I listened attentively to their feedforward, harvested valuable information, and collected inspiration. I think this is another form on a bigger scale of *Reverse Coaching*. I am a true believer in everyone's need for mentorship.

Patience, Firmness, and Tolerance

Leadership is both a science and an art. The science aspect comprises of the different theories and methods, whereas building the working environment to foster leadership and the flexibility in application reflects the art aspect.

Coaching and Developing Talent depends on people. Everyone has their unique strengths and weaknesses, different stages of development, and can change according to their surroundings. That is why effective leadership sometimes requires different levels of *Patience, Firmness, and Tolerance*.

While coaching, if you see an employee running into trouble, deviating from their task, making mistakes, or failing to meet a deadline, you should practice the virtue of *Patience*. Instead of criticizing the employee immediately for their problems, it is better to find the right time to gently remind them.

From seed germination to blossoming flowers to bearing fruit, the natural life cycle is a slow, long process, which parallels the growth of employees. Whether it is a new employee, an experienced employee, an inexperienced novice, a manager, senior manager, professional staff, etc., their learning and growth take time to mature.

When a child first learns how to walk, if its parents hold the child up immediately every time they are about to fall, the child will grow dependent on their parents and will never learn how to waddle on their own. Only with the *Patience* of the parents, who allow the child to make mistakes and try on their own, will the child be able to learn quickly.

Patience is the virtue of giving employees space to explore themselves rather than looking over their shoulder constantly. Within this supportive environment, employees will have a deeper understanding of their work, learn more, and gain confidence, which will improve their overall performance. This falls in line with the intentions of *Coaching and Developing Talent* and avoids the vices of power and control arising out of traditional leadership models.

Firmness refers to holding the highest standards when *Coaching and Developing Talent*. For example, when we run into a problem that has escalated into an issue of principle, we can no longer use *Patience* to face the matter and must instead use *Firmness*.

Without principles there will be no standards nor requirements. No one will be clear on what is right and what is wrong, what they can do, what they cannot, or what baseline they cannot cross. Once principles are violated, they will become more prone to future attacks, which would jeopardize the integrity of the entire company. *Firmness* is the attitude we should have in upholding our values.

In our company, whenever employees display unacceptable behavior according to our *Team Communication Model*, we promptly remind them to make corrections. When employees disrupt the flow of operations and cost the company major losses, we issue them a warning, hoping they can avoid repeating similar mistakes. When employees breach integrity, abandoning the company's ideals, we immediately ask them to leave.

Another important trait in being an excellent manager and coach is *Tolerance*. In my opinion, coaches should pay more attention to their staff because a manager's success stems from the growth and performance of the team.

This requires coaches to stand at a higher level, to see the big picture, and to direct everyone towards the future. They should also *Dare to Employ People More Competent than You*, help their staff improve, and allow them to become champions. This is what we call the *Tolerance* of a Coach.

An example would be giving employees an opportunity to stand on stage to receive applause and flowers while the supervisor cheers for them off-stage. A great supervisor will recognize their employee's contributions instead of taking credit for their own hard work. They will tolerate, encourage, and help their subordinates whenever they run into problems rather than blaming and getting mad at them. *Tolerance* allows a leader to balance between *Patience* and *Firmness*.

Exercising the three virtues of *Patience, Firmness, and Tolerance* is an art an effective coach should master. When to be *Patient*, to be *Firm*, to be *Tolerant*, all depends on the varying conditions at work. As long as we always *Focus on Intentions* while striving towards a *Common Goal*, we can master these virtues through reflection and practice.

Winning Mindset

As a coach, not only do you need to nurture your employees' skills, share your wisdom and experience with them, but also improve their morale, inspire them to pursue their dreams, and establish a *Winning Mindset*.

A *Winning Mindset* refers to the ideals of persistent breakthroughs and daring innovation. It encompasses the attitude to strive for the best, to pursue dreams, and to set more challenging goals each time around.

Having a *Winning Mindset*, employees will be more passionate, motivated to work, and will dedicate their enthusiasm and knowledge to the team. This attitude will improve employees' performance without the need for extreme supervision and monitoring.

Pure capability has its limitations, but combined with spiritual motivation, everyone can go a long way.

Just like playing on a football field, a coach always motivates the players to win, and to bring home the trophy. The faith and confidence in victory can inspire players to challenge themselves and push their limits to play the best match their audience has ever seen.

Our company has a dream, which is to create history and become China's and the world's number one health product company. We established this dream during our second five-year plan in 2005. At that time, the company's development was on track, performance was good, but it remained at a comfortable status quo that neglected our future direction. If the company had continued on that road, it would have had great difficulty making any breakthroughs or even sustaining itself. However, after creating this unified dream, we raised our employees' standards and goals, motivated our staff, and invigorated our team. By involving them in creating history and making a difference in the world, everyone began to recognize the value in the meaningful work they were doing.

During *Coaching and Developing Talent*, we continuously utilize this *Winning Mindset* to inspire and challenge our employees. This not only pushes our employees to grow quickly, but also pushes the company toward healthy progress.

Facilitation Skills

Among the many methods of education, one type is one-way teaching, where students simply absorb information from their teachers' lectures. Another type is two-way teaching, in which the teacher raises questions and the students participate in interactive discussions. Which style would you prefer?

I believe many of you would prefer a teaching style that comprises of raising questions, having discussions, participating in interactive exchange—an active two-way education.

In *Coaching and Developing Talent*, we raised another style of education, one we call *Facilitation*. Supervisors raise questions to inspire their staff to brainstorm, clarify ideas, and find solutions to problems. This is contrary to supervisors simply giving out final answers or clear directions. Facilitators advocate two-way communication. They inspire cooperation and collaborative problem solving while narrowing the gap between themselves and their subordinates.

Facilitators should feel confident that their staff can use their own abilities to find the right answers. Quite often, people already have the knowledge and creativity within them. Coaches can help employees enhance their skills through facilitating their problem-solving process. This two-way interaction can make people feel respected and empowered as they realize their strengths and value, sparking personal development.

For example, we generally implement our corporate culture through a number of strategic planning workshops. The facilitator guides the group to avoid solely searching for the final answer and to refrain from dominating the discussion with personal views. Rather, we promote productive discussions that gather communal opinions. The facilitator's role is to encourage effective debate and inspire brainstorming in order to find an agreement and a plan of action.

When an employee raises a specific question or directly asks for my opinion, I usually ask them back, "What do you think?" In asking that question, I want to hear them express their own thoughts first before consulting others.

When my employees voice their opinions, I do not respond immediately and instead will continue to ask "What else?", with the aim of further unlocking their ideas to promote a deeper level of thinking in search of more possibilities.

Even when I have an initial personal solution to problems when making a final decision, I never dominate discussions with my thoughts until after I ask for any additional comments.

We promote this method of *Facilitation* to collaboratively plan and solve problems. We often use this approach for one-on-one meetings between supervisors and their subordinates, for internal training, and for daily operations.

Motivation

Every employee wants to receive affirmation and recognition. Proper acknowledgment, sincere *Motivation*, and an appreciative attitude can help employees build confidence. In gaining momentum and owning a sense of mission and responsibility, this mode of work could reveal greater gifts to reach higher goals.

As a coach, one of the most important responsibilities is to encourage others. *Motivation* supplies care, praise, and warmth, while it transmits respect, trust, and responsibility. The result is trust, power, and growth.

For example, when employees run into trouble and ask for help, what would you do? If you say impatiently, "You can't even complete the task and you come to me for help?", your employee will feel discouraged and their performance level will decline.

However, if you patiently listen, reassure, and care about your staff, even without specific advice or instructions, your employee will feel your support. This will restore their confidence in problem solving. In many cases, the attentiveness, praise, and *Motivation* from managers are all employees need to perform well.

Compared to those of other ethnicities, Chinese entrepreneurs are mostly more reserved, less expressive, and avoid giving praise or *Motivation* because they believe that employees doing a good job is a given. However, I very much hope that our company's employees can frequently receive motivation, and recognition and thrive in the following working environment:

When an employee feels frustrated and depressed, we might say, "Do not worry, tell me about it." When an employee has no confidence in a task they have to complete, we might motivate them by saying, "I trust you; you can do it." When an employee effectively deals with an unexpected event to retrieve the company's losses, we might say, "You've done a great job managing the situation, thank you for your hard work." When an employee gained progress through a new achievement, we might promptly give them praise, saying, "You are awesome, keep up the good work!"

Reinforcement can be a cordial conversation, an inspirational speech, a small card, a firm handshake, a few motivating words, an enthusiastic letter of congratulations, or a little gift. *Motivation* should be inspired by the spiritual inspiration rather than the materialistic. It also requires flexible adaptation and utilization.

We have been working hard to create this inspiring culture in our company. When we finish a big project, achieve some success, or realize a new breakthrough, we usually organize a variety of celebratory activities. When our employees excel in learning, innovation, corporate culture, and in other aspects, we recognize their hard work. With regard to great performance such as making a significant contribution to a project, we will honor the employee at our annual event.

Motivation nurtures talent. When our management level has mastered the art of motivating our staff, we believe that our team's atmosphere, morale, and effectiveness will greatly improve.

Endnote

1. Lombardo, Michael M; Eichinger, Robert W. *The Career Architect Development Planner (1st ed.).* Lominger Limited, 1996.

PART III

The Seven Inquiries of the
Autopilot Leadership Model

After reading the previous chapters in which we shared the four reasons and six elements of the *Autopilot Leadership Model*, we hope that everyone has a better understanding of the model and know that we have invested a lot of time developing, practicing, and gaining benefits from this model. In mastering the *Autopilot Leadership Model*, you will have figured out the secrets to becoming a "Best Employer" with a best golf score of 71.

I also believe that everyone has their own views and perspectives on the *Autopilot Leadership Model* and may even have specific questions. I think so because when we began developing this model, it raised very interesting results as well as a lot of questions. My colleagues noted the confusion and obstacles that arose when we tried to implement the model in our daily operations.

For example, does *Autopilot* mean that the leader does not need to care about anything and their employees can run the company by themselves? Does *Autopilot* only concern the leader and not the rest of the employees? When the work is delegated to all the employees, what responsibilities does the leader have? Is *Autopilot* a science or an art? Can other enterprises effectively utilize *Autopilot*?

These questions, thoughts, and misunderstandings are valuable because they help revise and improve *Autopilot Leadership*. Even after more than a decade of application in our company, there is still room to improve. In fact, the questions mentioned above were encountered during our implementation and may continue to resurface in the future. They persistently keep us thinking, exploring, and striving to create a better-established and complete model. So the less confusion and the more understanding there is, the better the effectiveness of the model.

In the following chapters I will set out my thoughts on these issues. On one hand, I hope it helps everyone gain a better understanding of *Autopilot*. On the other hand, I hope that my sharing will further inspire everyone to collaboratively help improve the *Autopilot Leadership Model*.

Chapter 10

Autopilot Leadership = Pilotless Leadership?

When you first hear about the concept of *Autopilot Leadership*, your initial thought might be that the business leader does not need to care about anything; the company employees are free to run the business.

This is a big misunderstanding. *Autopilot Leadership* is not the same as pilotless leadership. Like flying a plane in autopilot mode, even though you do not need to manually fly the plane, you still need a pilot to monitor the weather conditions, obey traffic rules, and steer the plane toward the correct destination.

I aspire to become an *Invisible Leader*, who can delegate operational work to my employees. But it still requires me to be the pilot of the company, to set its course, care about the *Coaching and Development of Talent*, and promote our corporate culture.

For our employees, *Autopilot Leadership* gives them enough power and space to complete their jobs without constantly having to report to someone. In many cases, they are allowed to make their own decisions on specific working approaches and have a great scope of autonomy.

This space and autonomy works only when complemented by a *High Trust Environment*, a *Common Goal*, *Effective Empowerment*, and many other mechanisms at work. Our employees clearly understand their own roles and responsibilities as well as their relationship with the company's *Common Goal*. Moreover, from gaining respect, acknowledgment, and trust, our employees feel a strong sense of accountability and naturally perform exceptionally.

In this context, constant supervision is not needed so that more energy can be focused on creating a collaborative atmosphere, going toward the right direction, and setting a shared purpose to service and support our staff.

During *Effective Empowerment*, we do not simply delegate jobs to our employees and completely neglect following up with their work. Rather, we use OPERA as a tool to clarify the wanted Outcome, set Parameters, define Effects, provide Resources, and entrust Accountability. Through this method, our employees make a commitment to their assignments, which we trust they will complete innovatively with flying colors before the deadline.

Our company is like many others, where we have personnel, administration, finance, and other departmental guidelines. In addition, we also use Standard Operating Procedure and Work Instructions. These are all adapted to guide, regulate, and support our staff in their daily operations.

Therefore, *Autopilot Leadership* is not pilotless leadership. It does not represent a leader who does not care or manage at all, nor does it let employees do whatever they please. In reality, it is drawing large parameters for our staff to discover their talents, make new discoveries, find their own direction, and complete their work in a timely and proficient manner.

Chapter 11

Is the *Autopilot Leadership Model* Only the Leader's Concern?

Some people say that *Autopilot* is a leadership model, and therefore it only concerns the leader and no one else. In fact, this is another grave misinterpretation. This model depends on the collaboration of all employees, requiring everyone's participation and support.

133

For example, in creating a *High Trust Environment,* if only the leader trusts the staff and there is no trust the other way around as well, or vice versa, then this *High Trust Environment* will never come into existence.

In another case, it takes just one person in the leader's team who does not trust anyone else, or is unwilling to cooperate with and support others, or avoids accountability to severely jeopardize the *High Trust Environment.*

This also applies to setting a *Common Goal.* A leader is not solely responsible for it; rather, the entire team must actively participate in reaching an agreement. The execution and implementation of a common objective does not only concern the leader as well because it relies on the concerted efforts and hard work of all team members.

Even if a single person does not support the company's *Common Goal,* this will jeopardize the realization of the shared objective. Ultimately, it not only hinders the leader of the group, but also all team members.

In the current business world, a lot of leaders are measured by their presence in their company. But under *Autopilot Leadership,* a company should be able to run effectively without the constant presence of the leader. All employees of a company must understand the concept in order to put this theory into practice. While someone who understands the concept will appreciate their leader's work behind the scenes, someone who does not understand may criticize the leader's lack of presence.

In *Coaching and Developing Talent,* everyone has the chance to become a coach, whether it is through *Peer-to-Peer Coaching* or *Reverse Coaching.* We never discriminate against rank. Leadership does not solely concern the leader of the company but is actually practiced at every level.

In addition, the many concepts of the *Autopilot Leadership Model*, such as *Trust Others First, Focus on Intentions, Lead by Example, Active Listening and Open Communication,* and *Appreciate Differences,* not only help with work, but also improve and inspire everyone's families and personal lives.

Chapter 12

What Role Should the Leader Play?

The *Autopilot Leadership Model* removes the requirement of leaders doing all the hands-on work. It also dismisses constant close supervision and monitoring at the workplace.

In that case then, wouldn't leaders become irrelevant in the company?

On the contrary, *Autopilot Leadership* only allocates operational matters to a company's employees while allowing leaders to do what they were meant to and increase their leadership value to the company.

As the CEO of the company, after I assign specific tasks to others, I have more time and energy to focus on development strategies, long-term targets, advancement, and key projects for the year, such as employee satisfaction and corporate culture.

For example, in implementing corporate culture or discussing strategies, we need certain plans, where I will organize joint seminars to leverage off various colleagues to find a solution rather than brainstorm on my own. As another example, if the company wants to build a new plant, I will only concentrate on whom to delegate responsibilities to and what the target is. I will not concern myself with things like negotiations, design, construction, and other specific matters.

With this approach, as the CEO, I play the roles of an *Invisible Leader*, a strategist, and a coach instead of the executor, supervisor, or commander.

Therefore, I hope that leaders of companies can stop spending all their energy on operational issues, and instead put more time and effort in selecting, effectively deploying, and coaching talent. They should lead by example in implementing corporate culture, advocate corporate values, and be role models in embodying those principles. They should encourage their team members to pursue more challenging goals, amplify their dreams, build faith, inspire talent, and achieve significant performance. Moreover, they should concentrate on the company's overall development, operational systems, and its future.

In the mode of *Autopilot Leadership*, leaders should stop managing and start leading. Instead of handing over all the responsibilities to their employees and crossing their own arms, a leader should stand from a higher perspective to see further. While giving the employees space to perform, the leader should provide guidance, formulate strategies, and motivate others around them.

Chapter 13

Is the *Autopilot Leadership Model* a Science or an Art?

Some people may ask: "If *Autopilot* is a leadership model, does that mean it is a science?" And some others may ask in return: "Since *Autopilot Leadership* concentrates on people, then shouldn't it be a form of art instead of a form of science?"

In my opinion, the *Autopilot Leadership Model* has both scientific and artistic sides. Science represents structure, rationality, standards, and systems, which are tangible measures. On the other hand, art embodies flexibility, sensitivity, balance, and grasp, which are the spiritual aspects.

The six interlinked elements of the *Autopilot Leadership Model* integrate over a decade of our company's experience as well as Western management ideas, such as OPERA. These systematic tools of *Autopilot Leadership* reflect its scientific aspect.

At the same time, *Autopilot Leadership* has its artistic side. Its core ideas from Lao Zi's (老子) *Dao De Jing (道德經)* and

The Art of War's (孫子兵法) Dao, Tian, Di, Jiang, Fa (道, 天, 地, 將, 法) symbolize the model's Eastern origins. In addition, other specific ideas like *Happiness, Appreciate Differences,* and *Motivation* symbolize humanity and spirituality.

While the model has both scientific and artistic sides, it is the synergy of both that makes *Autopilot Leadership* more all-rounded and practical. For example, our company aims to set clear and reachable sales targets, which require quantitative measurements. At the same time, the balance between challenge and accomplishment requires artistic judgment. While these objectives bring a certain degree of challenge to the table, they are also reachable and therefore motivate our employees to strive for them. In reality, we have often performed beyond the goals we have set, which strongly improves confidence, happiness, and productivity.

As another example, when employees make mistakes, we always correct them while keeping their feelings in mind. We like to focus on principles, standards, approaches to improvement, and communication methods as well as productive methods to improve. In helping new employees grow, we are *Patient* in giving them enough time and space to learn. We are *Firm* in coaching them in a timely fashion so as to avoid making the same mistakes. In creating an *Effective Team*, we are proactive and direct when communicating. We make sure that we focus on *Effects* and try to find the right opportunity and method in solving problems.

Therefore, *Autopilot Leadership* is neither pure science nor pure art. Science and art are unified as one, in which the two complement one another, leveraging off one another's advantages in order to maximize the model's effectiveness.

Chapter 14

One Size Fits All?

Some people may ask the following questions: "Our company operates on a very small scale and we are still in the startup phase—could we still use the *Autopilot Leadership Model*?"; "We are a manufacturing company—could we use the *Autopilot Leadership Model*?"; "We are not a company, but a social organization—could we use the *Autopilot Leadership Model*?"

I believe that for any variety of companies, *Autopilot Leadership* has certain principles and methods that are worth learning from.

With regard to a company's scale, normally small startups may completely focus on survival. Typically, they have very few employees, the owner has to roll up their sleeves to do hands-on work and they also have to make all the decisions.

Startups can choose and apply certain methods in the *Autopilot Leadership Model*. Good examples would be inviting employees to participate in decision making, or focusing on corporate culture fit when scouting for talent, or keeping the model's various virtues and attitudes in mind when improving effectiveness and productivity. It can still realize the true value of *Autopilot* at this stage.

Autopilot Leadership also applies to bigger firms with tens and hundreds of employees and expanded market share, to the firm's advantage as well. Otherwise, a traditional bottleneck problem may arise if the owner is the sole person in charge of hiring, processing documents, and making all decisions.

As a company grows, so must its management system. With growing scale, there is a need for a different way to manage its complexity. *Autopilot Leadership* is one useful model to effectively engage employees. For example, by utilizing the *Inverted Triangle*, we can specifically motivate front-line personnel as they are closest to our customers. This can help us feel the pulse of the realities of market changes. Hence, their expertise can help the company to break through the bottleneck situation.

Therefore, the effectiveness of the *Autopilot Leadership Model* varies wildly from small, to medium, and large enterprises.

Of course, trust is the most important building block of the *Autopilot Leadership Model*. No matter what type of business, industry or organization, without trust, an owner has to do everything themselves. With an untrusting leader, employees do not have space to unleash their potential and will not contribute and perform at their best. This sort of mistrusting environment does not provide positive conditions for *Autopilot Leadership*.

Employees gain happiness from unlocking their talents: the company can attract the right talent and sustain its business— these successes are the main motivations for implementing *Autopilot Leadership*. I believe all owners and their enterprises pursue these accomplishments. Hence, no matter how large the organization, in the manufacturing or in the servicing sector, a business, social organization, or a governmental body, I urge everyone to try and adopt the *Autopilot Leadership Model.*

Every model or theory has its own character as well as its own implementation approaches. I believe it will work only if you want it to work. Ultimately, you have the power to change the status quo, to sustain this *Autopilot* working style, and to persevere.

Chapter 15

What are the Key Points in Implementing the *Autopilot Leadership Model*?

Regarding this question, my colleagues and I have diverse ideas, but there is no standard answer. I believe that interesting results may arise when everyone's ideas are presented.

Some believe that a good leader must *Lead by Example* for effective implementation of the *Autopilot Leadership Model*.

Therefore, if a leader only promotes *Autopilot Leadership* in words, but not in practice, no one will believe in this model. Moreover, if the leader interfered frequently with subordinates' work, the team will not feel *Effectively Empowered*. *Autopilot Leadership* will just be empty words.

Some others believe that the key is for the general staff to understand and to correctly apply the model.

Let's say a leader empowers their employees, clarifies all the elements of OPERA, and sets up the fundamentals of *Autopilot*

Leadership. If the subordinates do not truly understand the model, they will report endlessly, wait for instructions, and fail to work on their own. In this case, *Autopilot Leadership* will not have been effectively implemented.

Some think that the answer to implementing *Autopilot Leadership* is to build the theory into the corporate culture.

A company that builds a culture around *Autopilot Leadership* can attract talent. Subsequently, their conception of it, their philosophies, and their behavior will unite naturally rather than having external pressures enforcing *Autopilot Leadership's* principles. Despite the different backgrounds, industry, and experience of new employees, this culture will never change, like the spicy hot pot broth. New and old employees will be able to put in their best efforts and *Autopilot Leadership* will be effectively implemented.

Some have also said that the key to *Autopilot Leadership* is action.

No thoughts or words can speak louder than actions. No better model can hold any meaning if it is not truly implemented. *Autopilot Leadership* must be put into practice in order to uncover its true value.

Others have said that *Autopilot Leadership's* secret ingredient is everyone's participation.

The owner will take the lead to influence their managers; the managers will affect their subordinates; the transfer of knowledge will travel from top to bottom. This approach includes everyone and avoids any blind spots in implementation. Therefore, *Autopilot Leadership* should not simply be a managerial concern. It requires everyone's participation, support, and promotion to be fully realized.

In fact, these ideas and opinions are all justified in their own way. Every link and step is very important to implementing *Autopilot Leadership*. Companies in different stages of development or different departments may have variations in launching and applying the *Autopilot Leadership Model*.

Chapter 16

What is the Future of the *Autopilot Leadership Model*?

As I described in the first part of this book, the *Autopilot Leadership Model* has experienced constant trial and error, practice, review, and refinement for continual improvement.

Initially, our model had four mindsets, five reasons, and six elements. Later, to simplify, we cut it down to four reasons and six elements.

We also call *Autopilot* a "Leadership Model" instead of a "Management Model" when we further analyze the concept. We ultimately refused the label of "management," because it implies control. This meaning goes against our belief of giving others space to grow and unleash their potential strengths. Therefore, "management" and *Autopilot Leadership* do not exactly match with each other and "leadership" is a better fitted expression.

Our promotion of the *Autopilot Leadership Model* and our methods have also gone through major transformations.

There was a time we deemed advocating *Autopilot Leadership* the sole responsibility of our human resources department. Thus, everyone waited for the HR department's instructions and followed accordingly. Eventually, we found that everyone had a different interpretation of *Autopilot Leadership* and gradually major conflicts came about. Frequently, the concept was only promoted on the surface or verbally, but was never realized in action. Since no one could experience the benefits of *Autopilot Leadership,* no one felt the need to promote it, and the effectiveness of the model declined dramatically.

Later when we realized the dilemma in hand, we reflected and analyzed the situation collectively to solve the issue. Successfully, we encouraged everyone to implement *Autopilot Leadership* in daily operations and share what they had learned. As a result, this inspired enthusiasm for the model as everyone had worked through its advantages and disadvantages. This experience reinforced the learning, practicing, and coaching components of the *Autopilot Leadership Model.*

In the future, we will also set up an Autopilot Leadership Lab (ALL) to co-create and explore the future model of leadership. If anyone has comments, feedback, or questions, please feel free to email us at info@allab.com.

Perhaps we will further simplify its contents, allowing it to become more easily understood, remembered, and utilized. There is still room for improvement and we hope that we will be able to strive for a more refined version as well as make it more accessible for universal use.

Some might say that not all of the contents of the *Autopilot Leadership Model* originated from our company. I completely agree. The *Autopilot Leadership Model* is an integration of the best theories in management history that we have selected based on their usefulness and applicability to our company, which eventually took shape as this model. It is a flexible concept that can be easily transformed and reconstructed for specific application. As long as we pinpoint appropriate new elements to include in our model, we will integrate them to create a more inclusive and relevant tool for companies around the world.

However, regardless of all the changes, the soul of the *Autopilot Leadership Model* will always remain the same. It will always be inspired by the aspiration of attaining Lao Zi's (老子) *Invisible Leadership*, by the potential to unlock everyone's hidden strengths and values, and by striving to create history.

I believe that the future changes to the *Autopilot Leadership Model* will continue to inspire employees to leverage off others' wisdom and perfect the practice. This journey of discovery itself reflects the process of the *Autopilot Leadership Model*.

We hope that in the future, *Autopilot Leadership* will not only help our company, but also help other enterprises around the world to achieve sustainable development and everlasting excellence.

PART IV

The Culture and Mission Behind the *Autopilot Leadership Model*

After understanding the *Autopilot Leadership Model*, perhaps many readers will ask, "*Autopilot Leadership* has a relatively complete theoretical system with many examples and case studies. It is indeed a very interesting leadership model. But how can we successfully implement it?" In this section, I will introduce aspects of the corporate culture of Lee Kum Kee and Infinitus, such as our core value of *Si Li Ji Ren (思利及人), Constant Entrepreneurship*, and our mission.

The *Autopilot Leadership Model* did not appear from nowhere. Its founding, development, and implementation were a process. It especially traces its roots to our business' cultural and historical background.

The origin of *Autopilot Leadership* stems from Lee Kum Kee's 126-year-old management practices and the company's *Si Li Ji Ren (思利及人)* core value. The model's contents and implementation go hand in hand with *Constant Entrepreneurship*. Its future runs side by side with our corporate mission.

Autopilot Leadership also has an even deeper historical and cultural context. Regardless of whether it is *Si Li Ji Ren*

(思利及人) or the *Autopilot Leadership Model,* these concepts grew from the influence of traditional Chinese culture and wisdom. Eastern philosophy has nurtured our exploration and practice of these two key notions.

Chapter 17

Si Li Ji Ren and
Autopilot Leadership

There are many facets of life that define a person's true identity, such as religion, culture, norms, and laws. Similarly, Lee Kum Kee and Infinitus have been defined by the core value of *Si Li Ji Ren (思利及人)*. Furthermore, the formation and effective implementation of the *Autopilot Leadership Model* build on top of this core value.

The four words, *Si Li Ji Ren (思利及人)*, always remind me of a story.

In the mid-20th century, my father Lee Man Tat encountered a calligraphy artist while he was traveling in Taiwan. The two found common ground and instantly became friends. To commemorate this unforgettable meeting, the calligraphy artist gave my father a calligraphy canvas that my father has cherished over all these years.

It wrote, "修身豈為名傳世, 作事惟思利及人." Translated into English, it means, "Doing good deeds should not be for a shining legacy, but for others' interests and the whole community's benefits." Inspired by the heartfelt message, my father captured the last four characters of this work of art and the core value of *Si Li Ji Ren (思利及人)* flourished. These four words are a reflection of the family business' values. It is a reminder to put the good of others in front of our own self-interest. It is the ideal way of life that we should all strive to attain.

Si Li Ji Ren (思利及人) is not a value that solely applies to a company; rather it can be a personal principle as well. Like a snowball effect, the more you consider others' interests, the more people are willing to help you, and ultimately the more successful your endeavors will become. A company will prosper, command respect and recognition from employees, partners, and the community only if it incorporates *Si Li Ji Ren (思利及人)* into its corporate culture. Life is full of reciprocal relationships, in which you can be helped when you help others.

When I was young, my father used to bring my siblings and me along to business meetings, exposing us to a diverse array of corporate environments. He always told us that heavy bargaining might result in one-time cut-rate deals. You might win in the first round of negotiations by reducing a one-time price, but in the many repeated rounds in the future, your collaborator might not even want to work with you anymore. Following that, in order to make a new business partner, you might increase your own costs. In the worst-case scenario, your business partner cannot make a profit and is forced to reduce their product quality to cut down on costs. Ultimately, you become the biggest loser. However, with a little give and take, a lasting relationship with business partners will guarantee long-term success. With a *Si Li Ji Ren (思利及人)* mindset, you can achieve greater success if you reflect on the good of others. This state of being and these lessons have always remained in my heart and mind.

Si Li Ji Ren (思利及人) is the main success factor of Lee Kum Kee being a company with such a rich history. This core value has three elements: *Helicopter View (直升機思維)*, *Think from Others' Perspectives (換位思考)*, and *Care about Others' Feelings (關注對方感受)*.

Helicopter View (直升機思維) alludes to a way of reconciling the relationship between the individual and the community. In going forward, we must take a step back and consider the big picture as if looking down from a helicopter. The farther away we are, the clearer and the more complete is our perspective, and also, the better the view.

Think from Others' Perspectives (換位思考) carries the same meaning as "Walking a mile in another's shoes." It signifies shifting your own perspective to get a clearer picture.

Last but not least, *Care about Others' Feelings (關注對方感受)* is important to your every word and action. The way you say something, what you say, and when you say it affect the way others feel. Understanding everyone's perspectives can sustain respect among each other.

Let me share a personal incident. In 1998, the shifts in China's governmental policies prohibited Infinitus from continuing its operations as before and the company needed to decide on whether to stay in business or to quit direct selling. This fight or flight moment led to a crisis management meeting, in which I expressed my main concern: "There are so many partners that depend on the success of Infinitus in order to survive, and moreover, most of them are family businesses. How would their livelihoods be affected?"

In times of adversity, we regarded the interests of our business partners as our top priority. Putting *Si Li Ji Ren* (思利及人) into practice, we respected our partners—their customers, experience, and hard work.

With *Think from Others' Perspectives* (换位思考), we finally reached a consensus and sent out a letter to all our partners and our employees the next day to announce our final decision. We were to stay in the game, stand by our company, change our model of operation, but remain loyal to our corporate culture and core values. We won everyone's support and trust. Not only did we survive but we also thrived during those turbulent times.

On a happier note, our company always organizes an annual award to recognize those employees who have excelled and shared their success with Infinitus. This ceremony is also a part of our *Si Li Ji Ren* (思利及人) slogan. We reward our employees for their hard work; their loyalty to the company grows, and ultimately, everyone persistently strives toward our shared purpose to achieve success. An employee once commented that working for Infinitus was just like working for their own company. This shows a tremendous sense of belonging and intimacy that employees hold close to their hearts.

The *Si Li Ji Ren* (思利及人) culture emphasizes the importance of people. It is imperative to keep others' benefits in mind, to stand in their shoes and to consider their feelings. With the *Autopilot* model, people are also the main emphasis. It alludes to the way individuals work within the context of a team, *Choosing the Right Talent, Unleashing One's Potential,* and achieving *Happiness,* which all point to the significance of caring about and respecting others.

Hence, the *Autopilot* model can only be fully appreciated through the comprehension and effective embodiment of *Si Li Ji Ren (思利及人)*. The three features of *Si Li Ji Ren (思利及人)* are imperative for the ideal to be achieved. We hope that our company and the people who work with us can embody these three hallmarks of our philosophy. By pioneering these habits, we hope to motivate both personal and corporate growth. We trust that with a strong backbone, our employees will be able to easily understand the intentions behind the various segments of *Autopilot Leadership,* apply the model, and realize it.

Chapter 18

Constant Entrepreneurship and the *Autopilot Leadership Model*

The spirit of *Constant Entrepreneurship* is Lee Kum Kee's key success factor in sustaining its progress for over 120 years. In Lee Kum Kee's dictionary, the notion of maintaining the status quo does not exist, but rather persistent and enduring entrepreneurship takes a major foothold in its place.

With the attitude of maintaining a business, we maintain a conservative outlook and feel comfortable with the status quo. Being afraid of or unwilling to try new things may make us miss opportunities to advance further. Without improvement and without development, our company will not be able to excel. While others move forward, we will fall back, so much so that we will lose the confidence of our employees and customers.

Therefore, like many other enterprises, we also advocate the entrepreneurial spirit at Infinitus.

Lee Kum Kee has had a tradition for well over 40 years—the annual spring event, Founder's Day. One year, we invited more than 8,000 employees and partners from around the world to participate in our event, which commemorates our ancestors, demonstrates our gratitude, and promotes *Constant Entrepreneurship*.

What is *Constant Entrepreneurship*? My understanding is that it means to maintain a winning mentality, to defy any limitations, to break through and innovate, and to try something you have never done before.

After Lee Kum Kee realized its first historical mission of "Promoting Chinese cuisines worldwide," the company did not stop there and instead developed a new goal and mission: "To promote Chinese preventive health culture to nurture more balanced, affluent, and harmonious lives." This is perseverance and *Constant Entrepreneurship*, which have instilled powerful passion and vitality into our century-old family business.

Under the spirit of *Constant Entrepreneurship*, we always pay attention to the changes in national policies, in society's lifestyles, in the industry, and in the market. In grasping the current terrain, we adapt accordingly, cooperate with the government, the media, and partners to leverage, integrate, and plan for the future to ensure progress is always on the way.

In our opinion, *Constant Entrepreneurship* has three important behavioral indicators: *6677, Dare to Try and Take Responsibility,* and *Encourage Innovation*.

6677 means capturing opportunities even when we only hold 60–70 percent certainty of success.

We think that one can never be 100 percent certain of anything. If there was such certainty, the opportunity would have been missed already. When I first entered the Traditional Chinese Medicine industry, my father and I traveled to Guangzhou to collaborate with Southern Medical University (at the time, named The First Military Medical University). Even though we had neither experience nor talent pool in this industry, we foresaw the potential of Traditional Chinese Medicine, the strength and reputation of Southern Medical University, and Lee Kum Kee's century-old brand and experience. With this in mind, we spent only an hour deliberating and grasped this opportunity. Thus, we began to develop the foundation of our business venture, creating Infinitus.

Being innovative always has its risks, but only through facing uncertainty and daring to take responsibility can we really make new breakthroughs. Therefore, we always encourage our employees to think outside the box and unlock their abilities in all our daily operations. This not only reflects the spirit of *Constant Entrepreneurship*, but also plays an important role in implementing the *Autopilot Leadership Model*.

It is not difficult to see that *Constant Entrepreneurship* and *Autopilot Leadership* complement each other. Their core ideology and principles are shared and their intentions are both to sustain the development of enterprises. In advocating *Constant Entrepreneurship*, we can mobilize the inner thoughts of our employees, and encourage them to keep up their good work, passion, and attitude. This complements the idea of creating a *High Trust Environment* from the *Autopilot Leadership Model*.

Hence, *Constant Entrepreneurship* and *Si Li Ji Ren (思利及人)* are the cornerstones of Infinitus, allowing *Autopilot Leadership* to build its strong foundation. With these two core building blocks, implementing *Autopilot Leadership* becomes much more successful, employees' support and comprehension become magnified, and the overall effects become more powerful.

Chapter 19

The Value of Eastern Wisdom in Modern Times

Others often ask me, is the *Autopilot Leadership Model* an Eastern leadership model, a Western leadership model, or a combination of both?

In my opinion, *Autopilot Leadership's* theoretical core is derived from traditional Chinese culture, especially the concept of the *Invisible Leader*.

Traditional Chinese culture requires us to think from the group's perspective, to avoid only pursuing personal interests. It emphasizes collective goals and synergizing our personal development with that of the entire society.

With regard to the *Autopilot Leadership Model*, people are the most important element because they affect policy formulation and goal achievement. If everyone feels cared for, respected, valued, and their needs are satisfied, then everyone can perform well with the immense energy and happiness that is within them. As we encourage personal development, we should also focus on team-building mechanisms, allowing everyone to challenge their limits, and to collaborate with united power to reach higher goals.

In addition, some other elements of the *Autopilot Leadership Model* originate from Chinese culture, such as the strategy of *Dao, Tian, Di, Jiang, Fa (道, 天, 地, 將, 法)* from *The Art of War (孫子兵法)*. Moreover, *Lead by Example* and *Choosing the Right Talent* also come from the conventional wisdom of Chinese culture.

Therefore, in essence, the *Autopilot Leadership Model* is an Eastern model based on Eastern philosophy and culture.

In the knowledge and service economy of the 21st century, traditional Eastern wisdom will continue to play a significant role. Research into and application of Eastern wisdom is becoming a trend in corporate management. *Autopilot Leadership* is one example that is rooted in Eastern philosophy, striving to share this wisdom with the rest of the world and make a difference.

However, there is no doubt that the *Autopilot Leadership Model* draws advanced management methods from the West. Western styles of management put more emphasis on systems and processes—Western-style management models ensure every detail is standardized and routine to create systematic results. In the past century, from Taylor to Drucker, many have created management theories like assembly line production to streamline manufacturing, Six Sigma, Enterprise Resource Planning (ERP), the balanced scorecard and other management tools. Western management theories have led the development of contemporary enterprises for the past few centuries with ongoing innovations.

Hence, despite the Chinese core of the *Autopilot Leadership Model*, many of its ideas and practices come from the West or from all around the world, especially the quantifying and institutional tools. For example, the empowerment tool of OPERA is a classic Western management method. Our company's modern governance system encompasses *Autopilot Leadership*, exemplified by our board, managerial structure, organization, and financial and personnel systems.

Therefore, the *Autopilot Leadership Model* is derived from traditional Chinese culture and Eastern wisdom, but also incorporates some modern Western management methods. With innovative management concepts and methods from the 21st century, I believe that the *Autopilot Leadership Model* will not only benefit Chinese enterprises, but also bring greater value to companies all around the world.

Chapter 20

Being a Mission-driven Company

To have a sense of mission is critical to all companies and Lee Kum Kee is a mission-driven company with a dream.

My great-grandfather Lee Kum Sheung invented oyster sauce in 1888 and created his own business, the brand of Lee Kum Kee, which has survived and prospered for over 120 years.

Up to now, the brand of Lee Kum Kee has endured in the past three centuries to become one of the oldest Chinese enterprises known to the world. Moreover, Lee Kum Kee has broken the Chinese curse of wealth not lasting more than three generations as I represent the fourth generation of the family business. While the business continues to expand and influence the world, I hope that Lee Kum Kee can become a model for other family businesses in the future.

The first historical mission of Lee Kum Kee is to promote Chinese cuisines worldwide. Traditional Chinese food culture is vast and dense, and Chinese restaurants have enjoyed a favorable reputation around the world. Lee Kum Kee strives to promote this mission through the production and sales of condiments. To date Lee Kum Kee has over 200 kinds of sauces sold to over 100 countries and regions. In many supermarkets in Europe and America, you will find the brand Lee Kum Kee, which gives Chinese people a sense of warmth and pride. You could say that Lee Kum Kee successfully achieved its first historical mission through sharing these products with the rest of the world while building its brand as a Chinese enterprise.

Lee Kum Kee's second historical mission also relates to traditional Chinese culture, namely, to promote Chinese preventive health culture to nurture more balanced, affluent, and harmonious lives.

China's preventive health culture of over 5,000 years has left a profound mark on the history of the nation. It has enhanced health and cured illnesses, allowing descendants to thrive and make contributions to the country. It has empowered Chinese people to struggle through a variety of disasters with strong vitality. Although modern medicine has made its immense progress and Western medicine has become the mainstream ideology, traditional Chinese medicine is growing and holds great promise.

We also hope that traditional Chinese culture and other cultures around the world can synergize in forming a unique leadership model that we can share with others. In parts of the west local enterprises have somehow absorbed the wisdom of traditional Chinese culture, such as *The Art of War* (孫子兵法), while developing their system of operations and corporate culture. On the other hand, the East adopts many Western ideas as well. Our model has integrated both.

In the contemporary world, as emphasized by traditional Chinese culture, we should become people-oriented, master the wisdom of winning people's dedication, and grasp the means of effective encouragement. By combining all this knowledge, we should be able to perform with flying colors. Following the dominance and influence of management studies from the United States, Europe, and Japan, China should also share its 5,000 years of experience and wisdom with the rest of the world and contribute more management ideas and models to the global business community.

Lee Kum Kee is a business of four generations that sets itself up as an example for others in terms of business philosophy. The company perpetuates its Chinese heritage with pride as a progressive and sustainable family business. We hope that more people will share and exchange ideas about the *Autopilot Leadership Model* we have developed to inspire others to embrace the strengths of Chinese culture, and to collaborate with other like-minded enterprises to create more value and make history on behalf of Chinese society.

We are striving to fulfill this mission.

Having a sense of mission lets us magnify our dreams, reach for higher goals, and challenge ourselves. Being mission-driven forces us to grow stronger, and go farther.

Whether it is *Si Li Ji Ren (思利及人)*, or *Constant Entrepreneurship*, or the *Autopilot Leadership Model*, in my opinion they were all brought together by traditional Chinese wisdom and Western methods. More importantly, this wealth of knowledge does not solely belong to us. Rather, it belongs to society as a whole. I believe that this knowledge can carry forward traditional Chinese culture, and help realize personal, corporate, national, and ethnic progress. I earnestly wish that the ideas in this book create value and change the world for the better.

Index